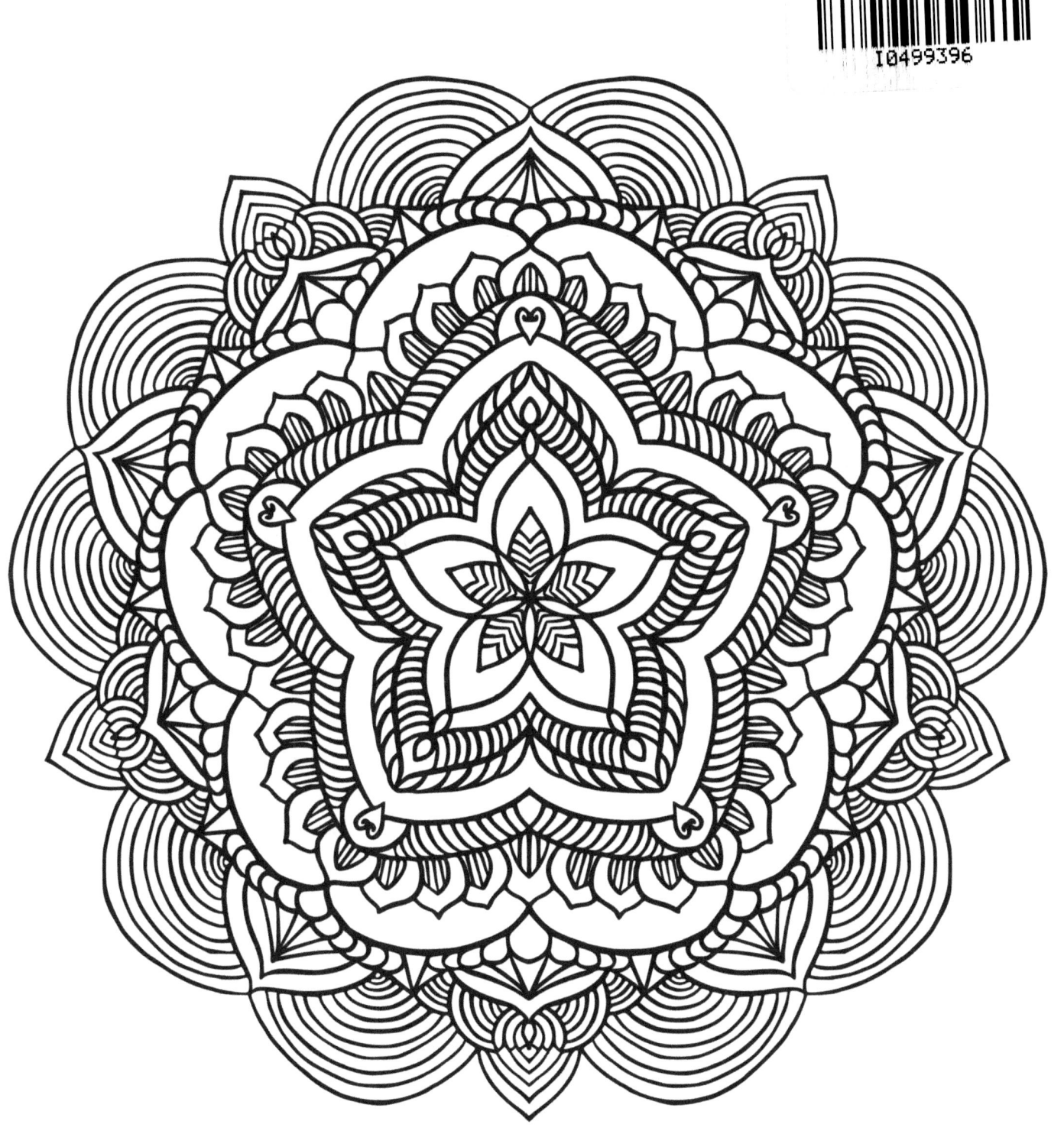

I hope you find some peace between these pages

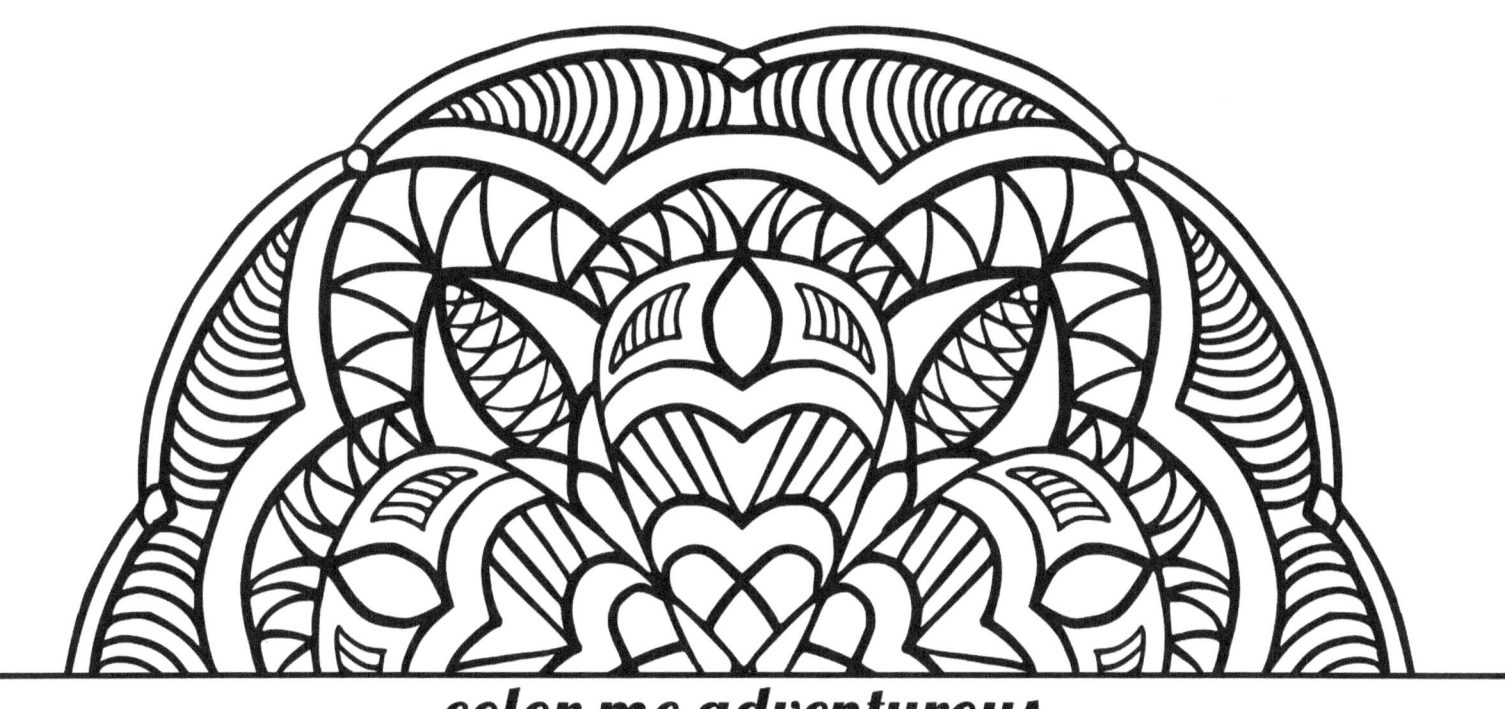
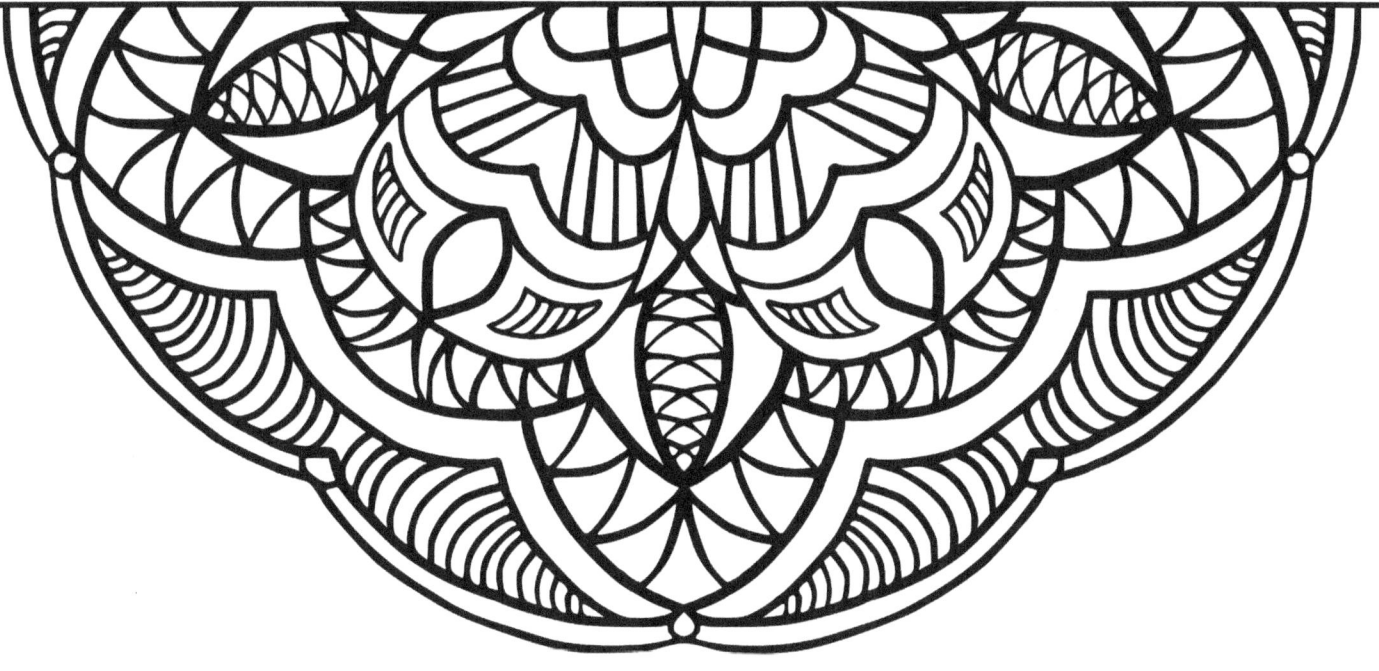
color me adventurous

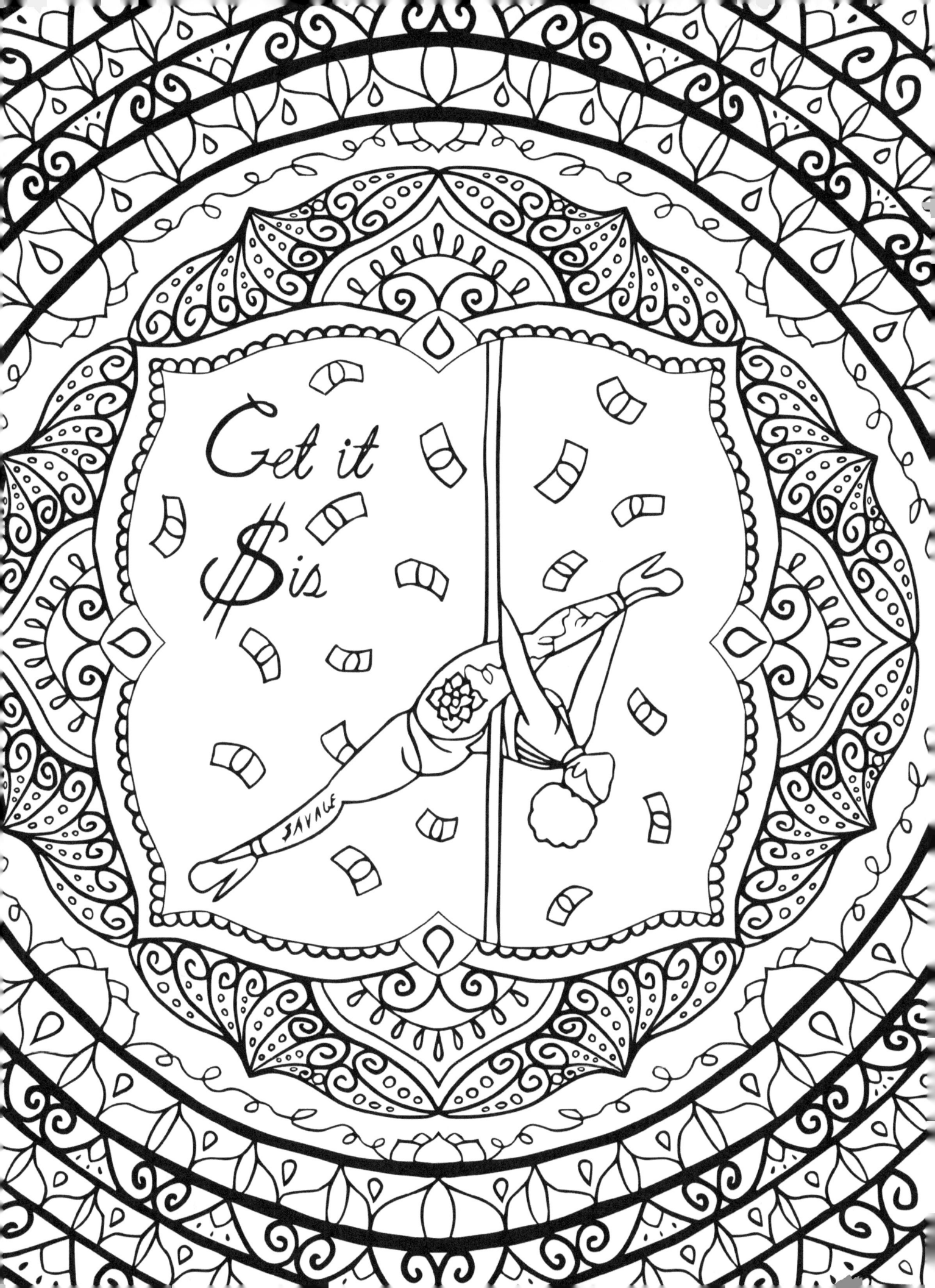

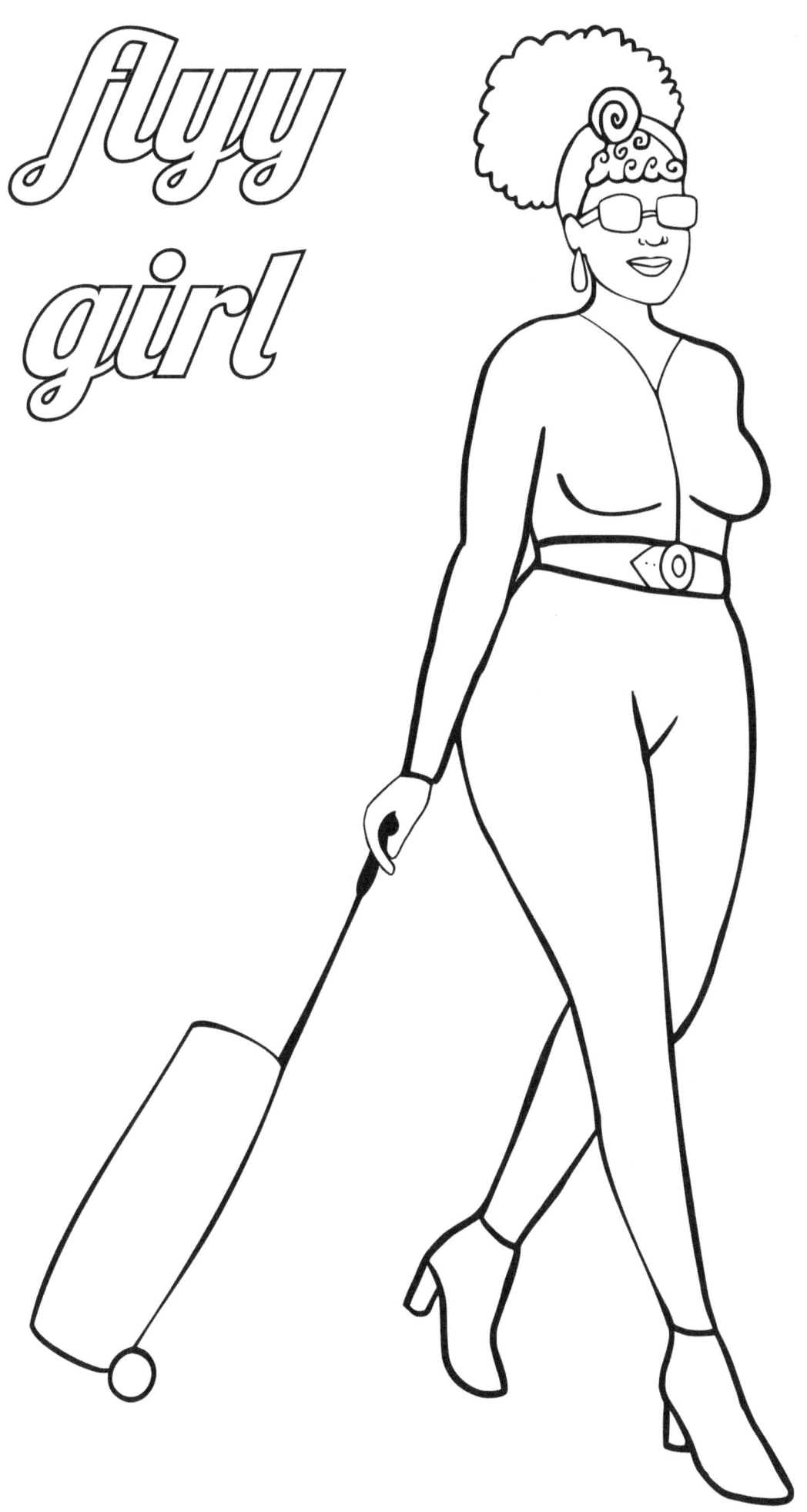

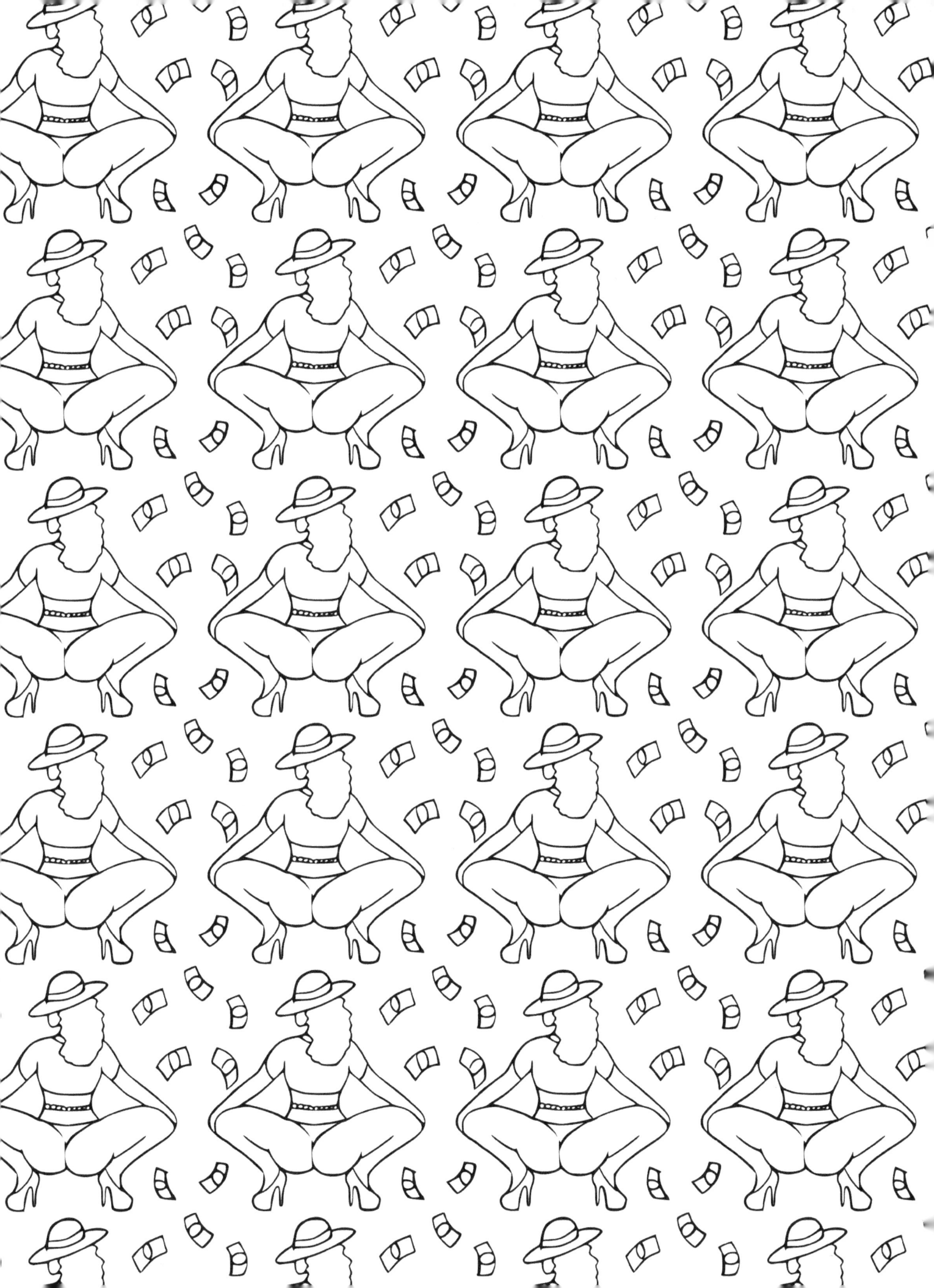

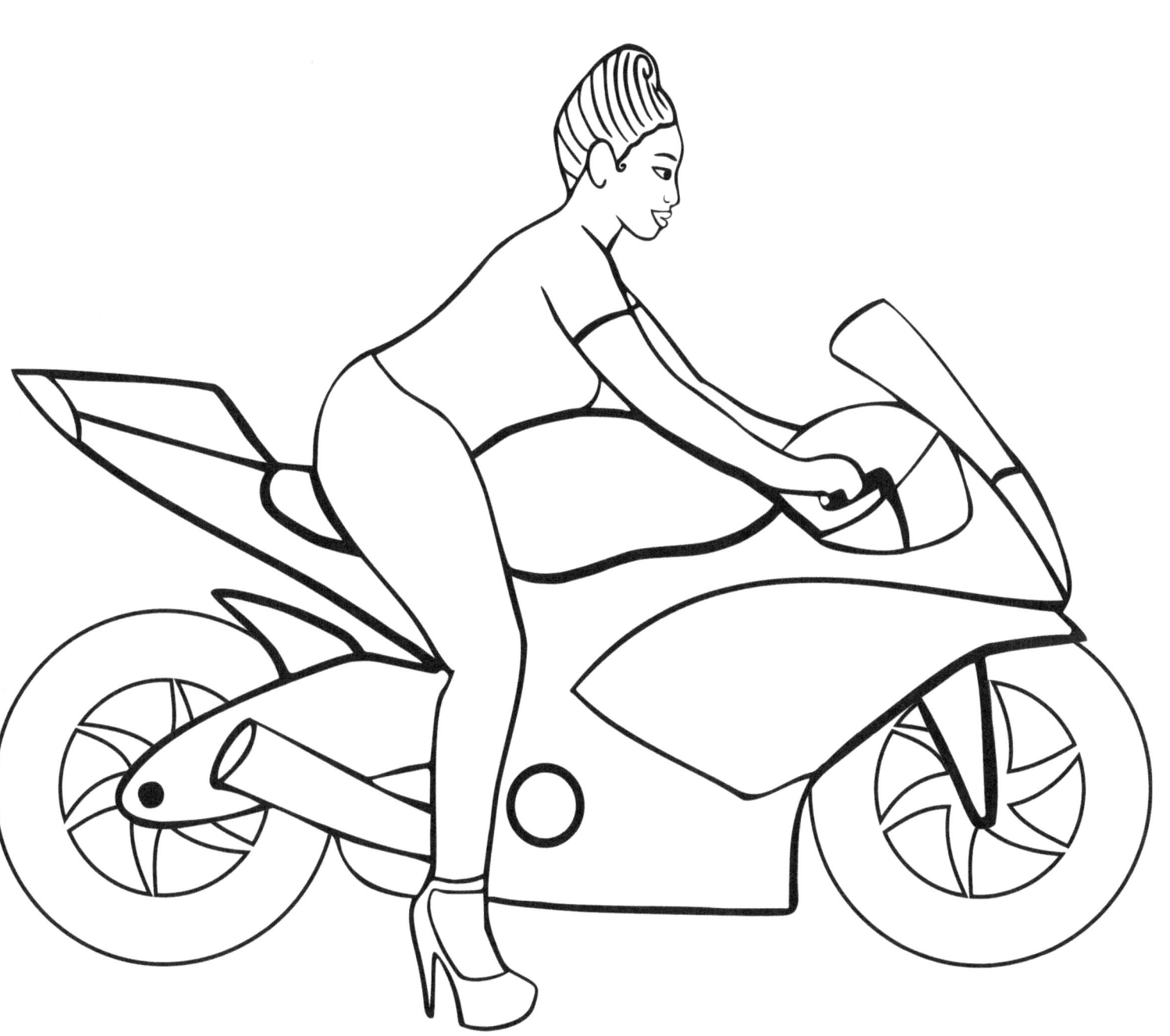

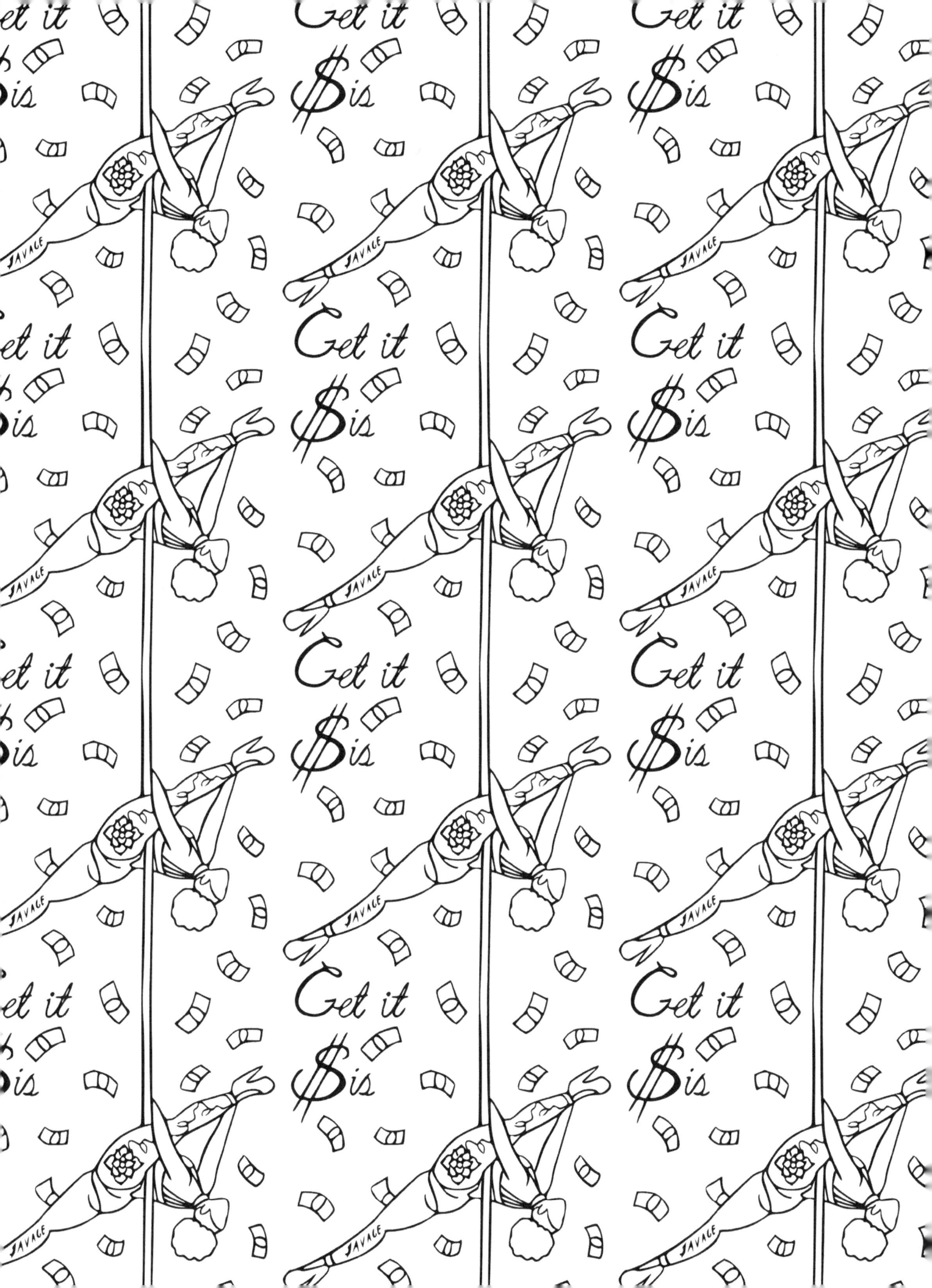

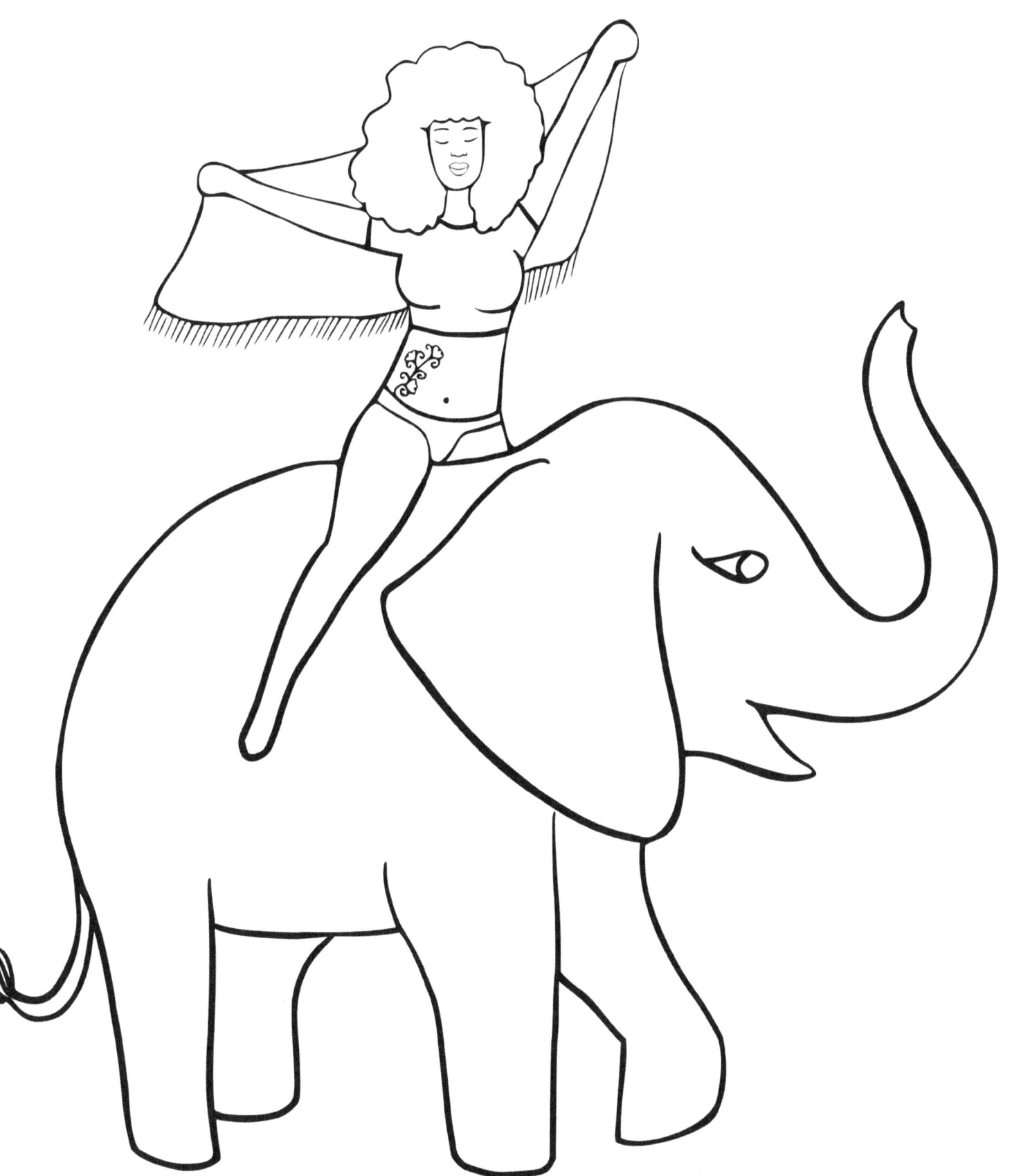

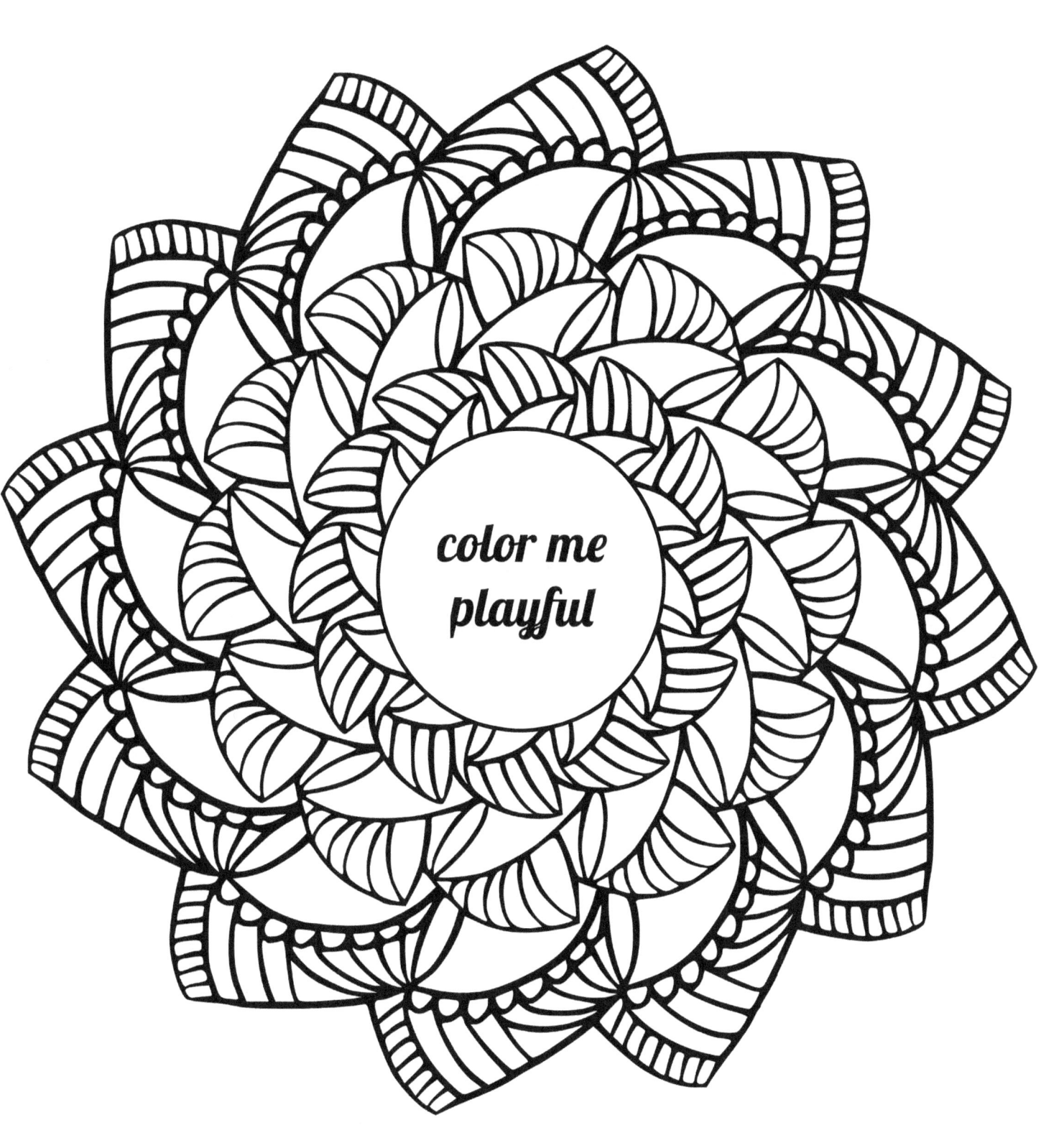

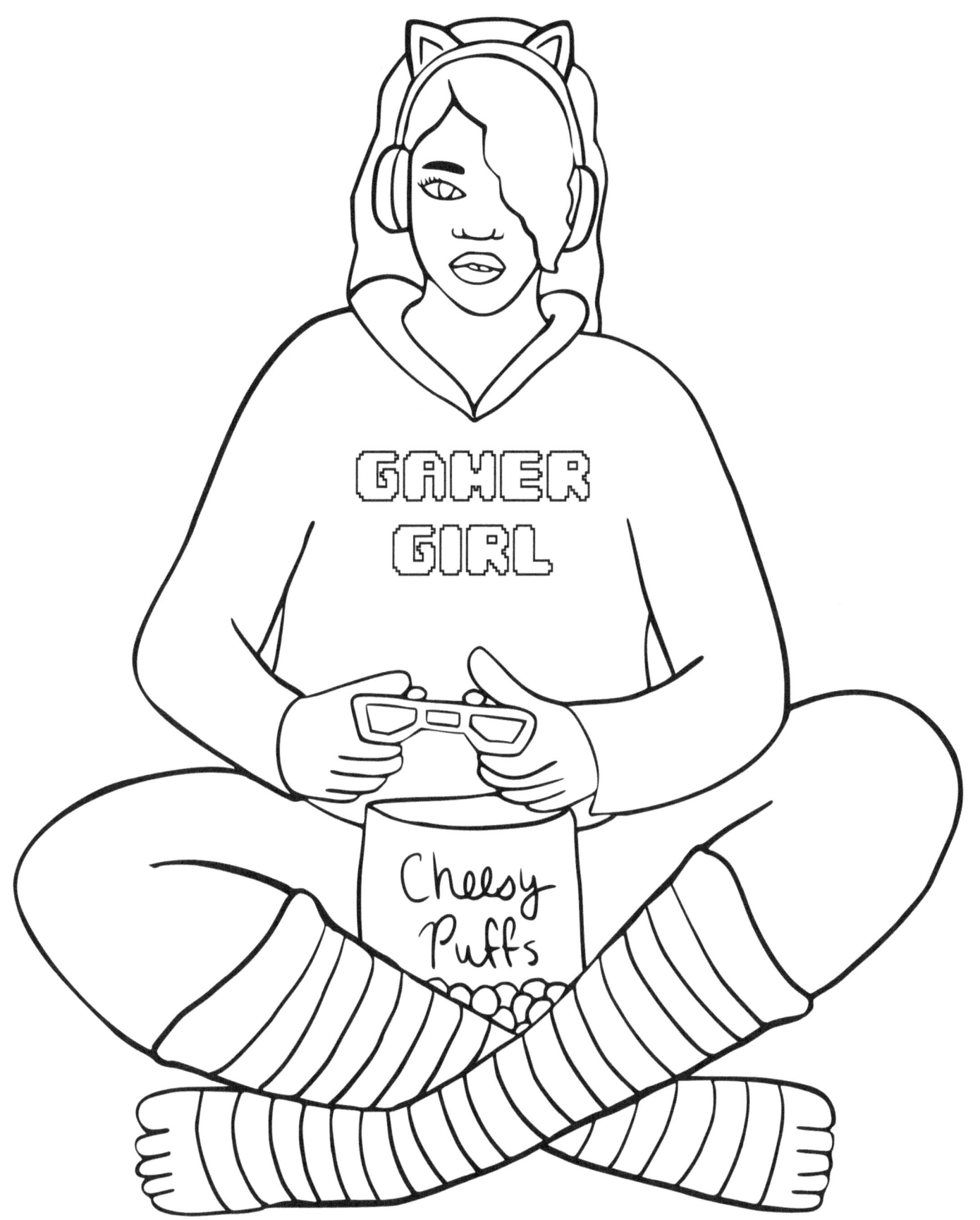

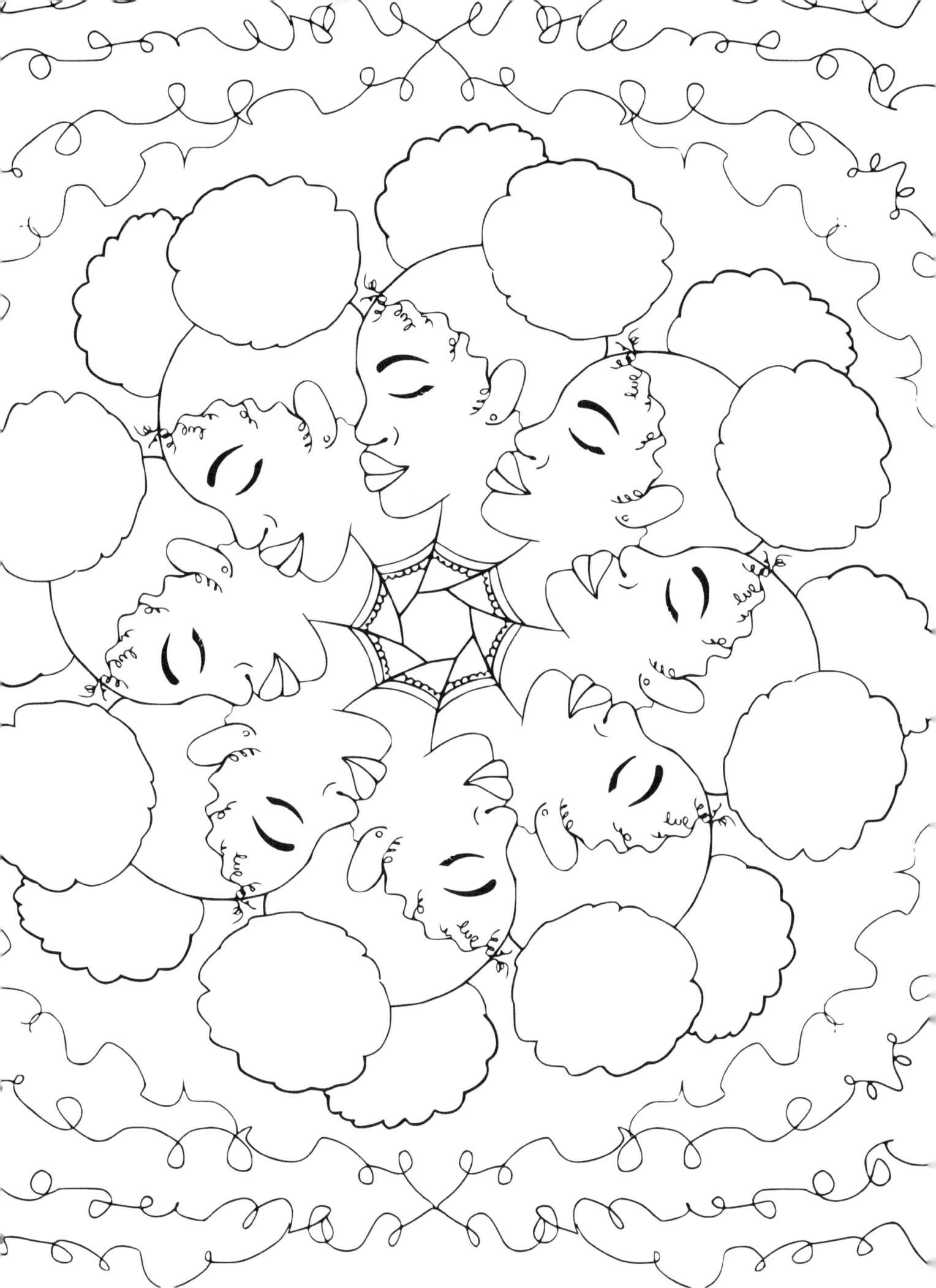

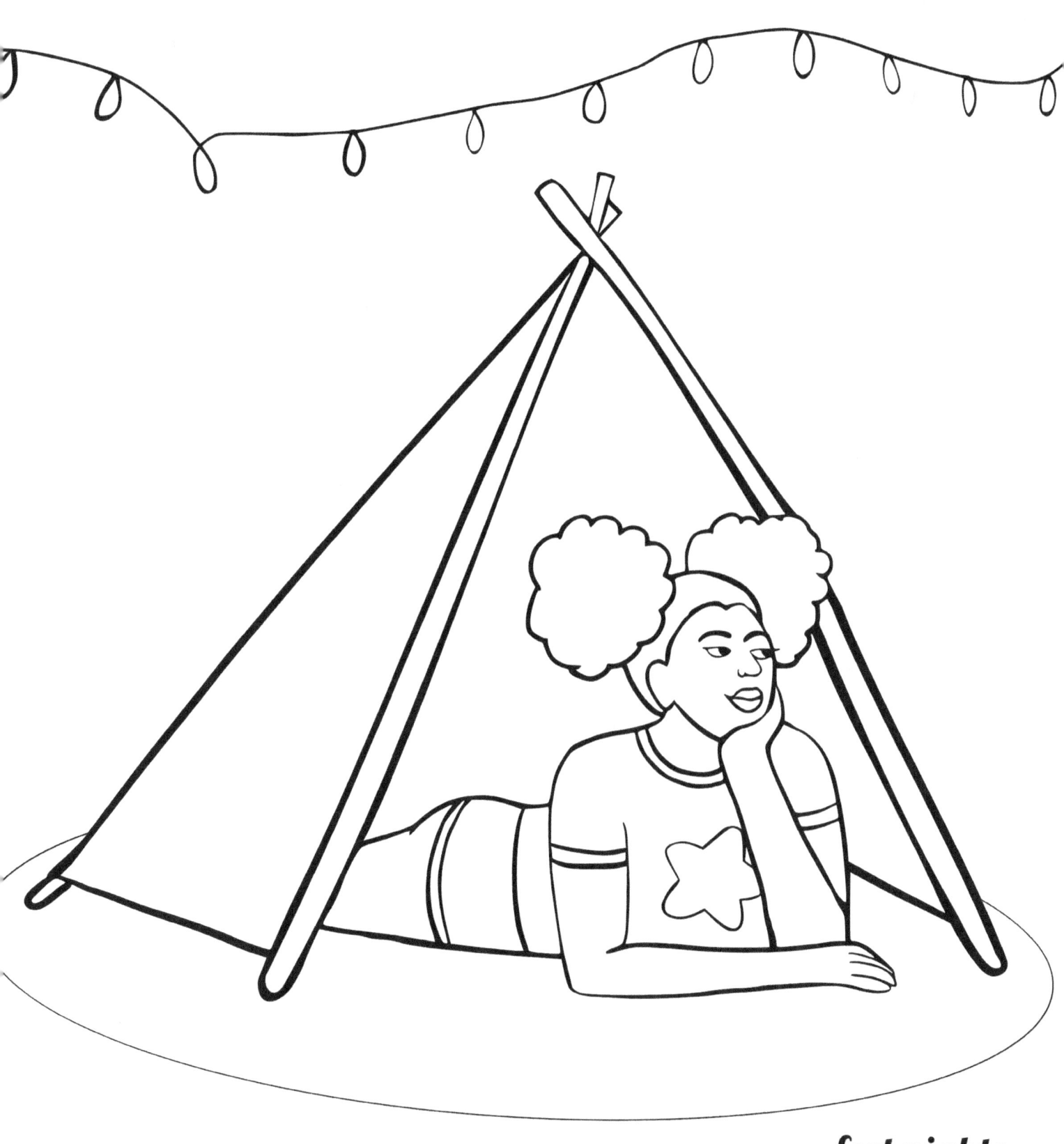

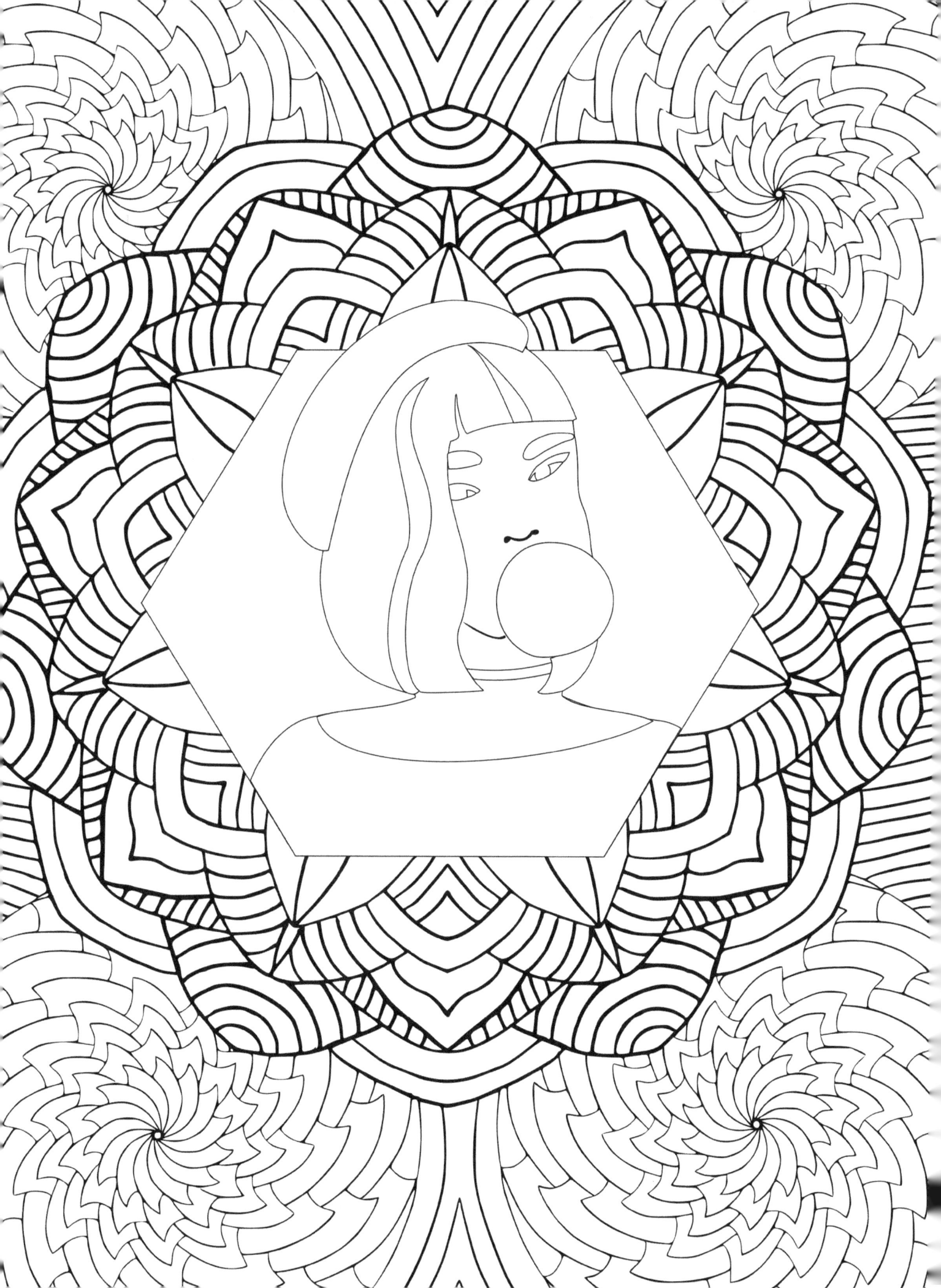

Cosplay cutie

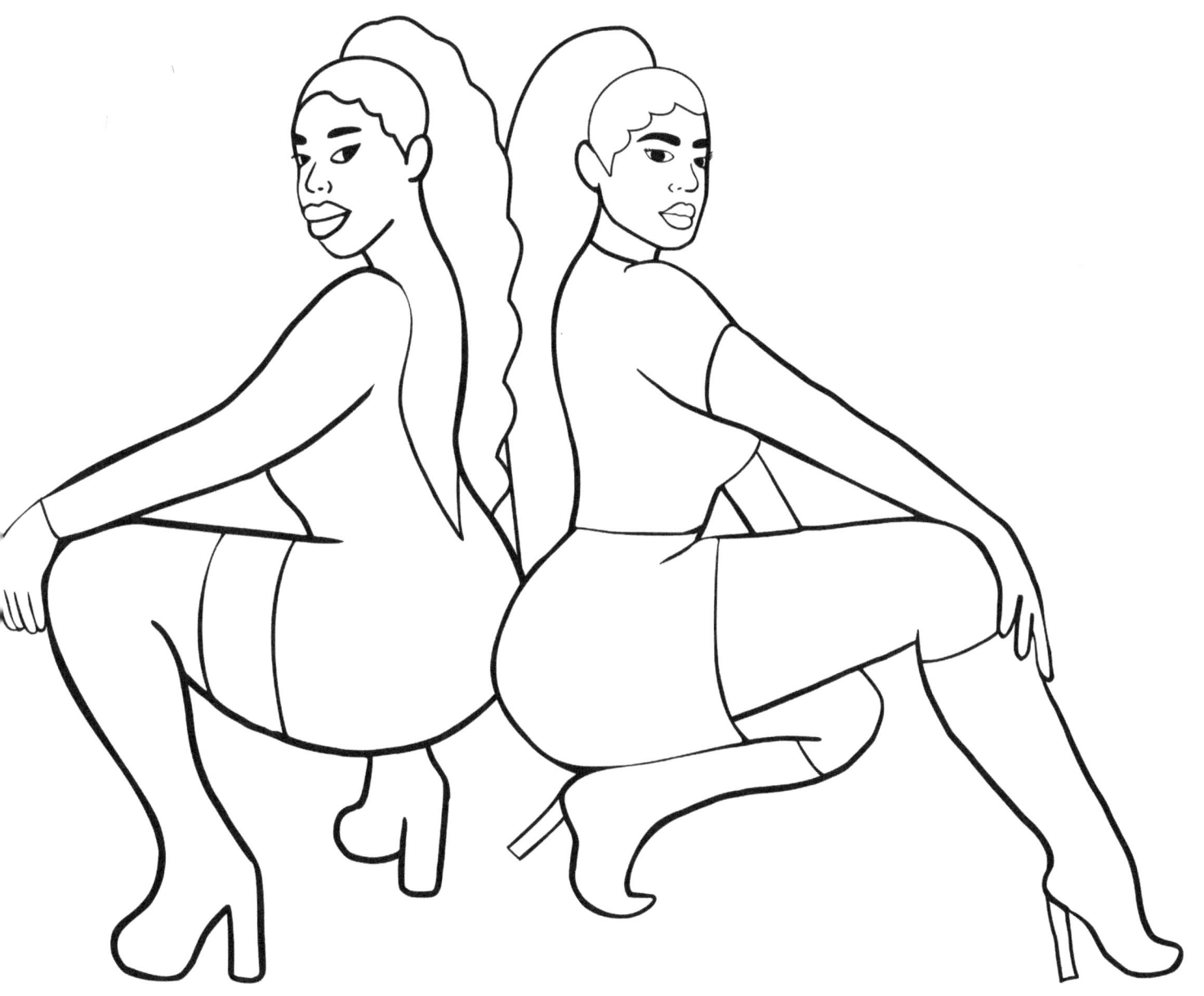

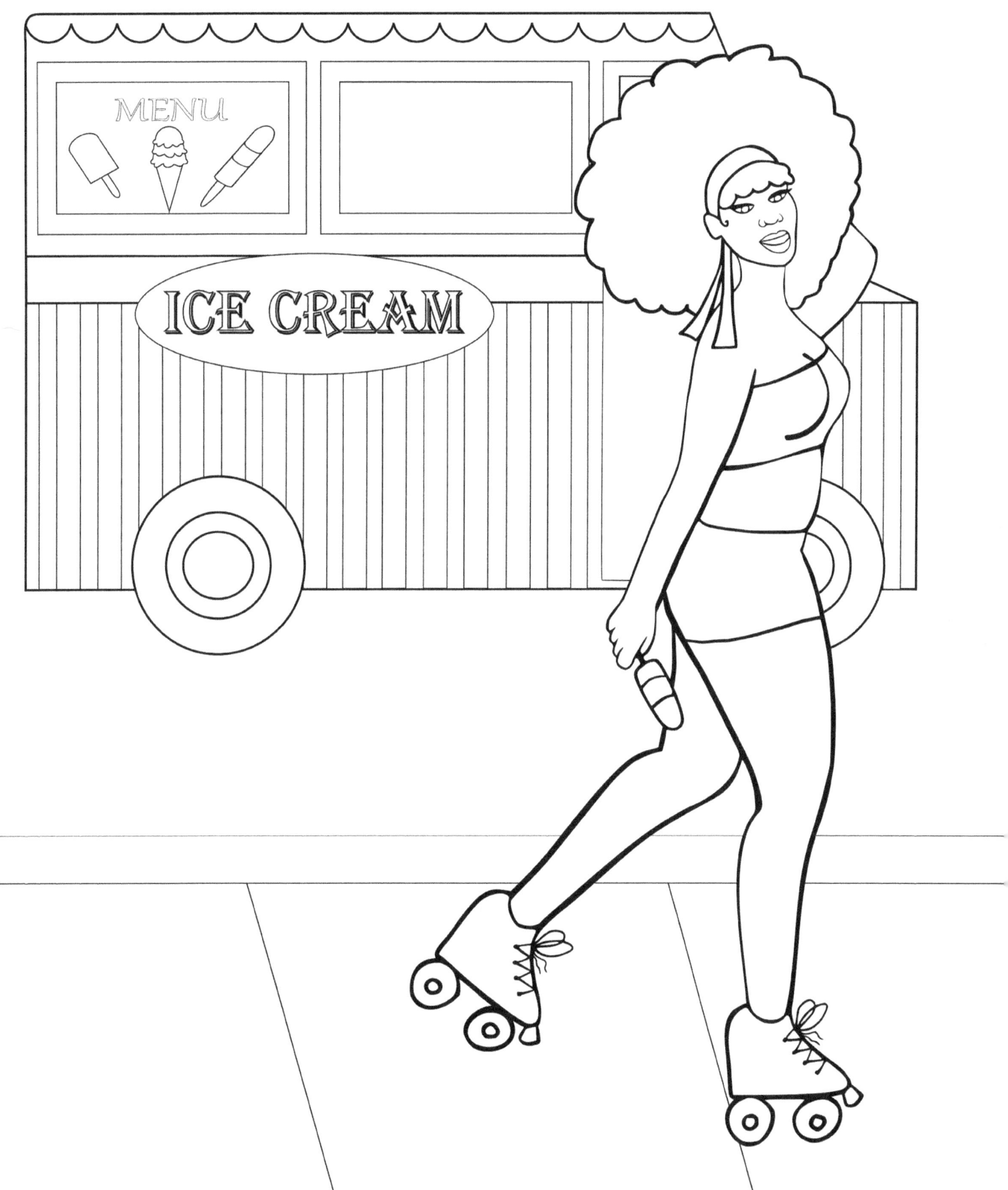

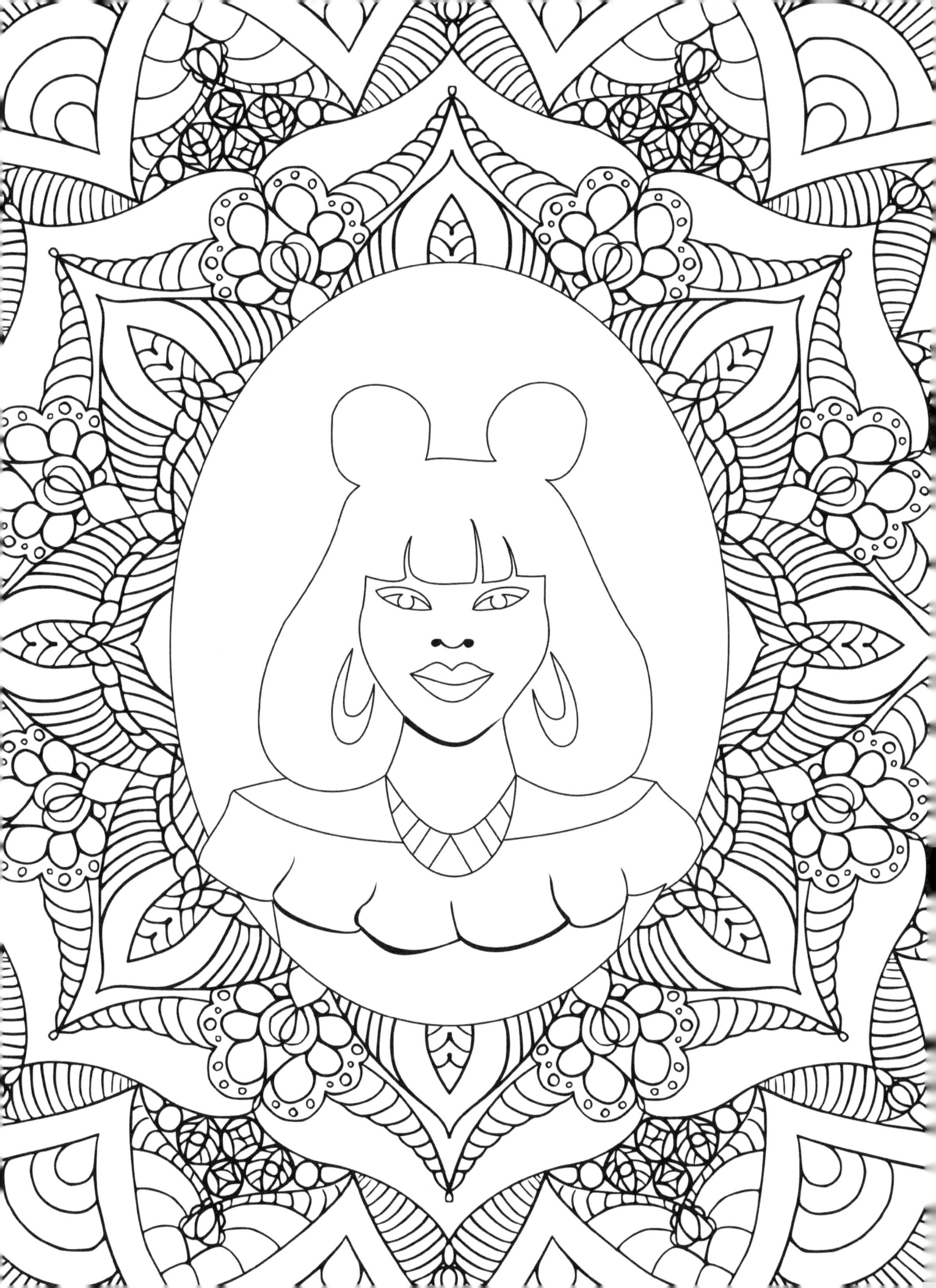

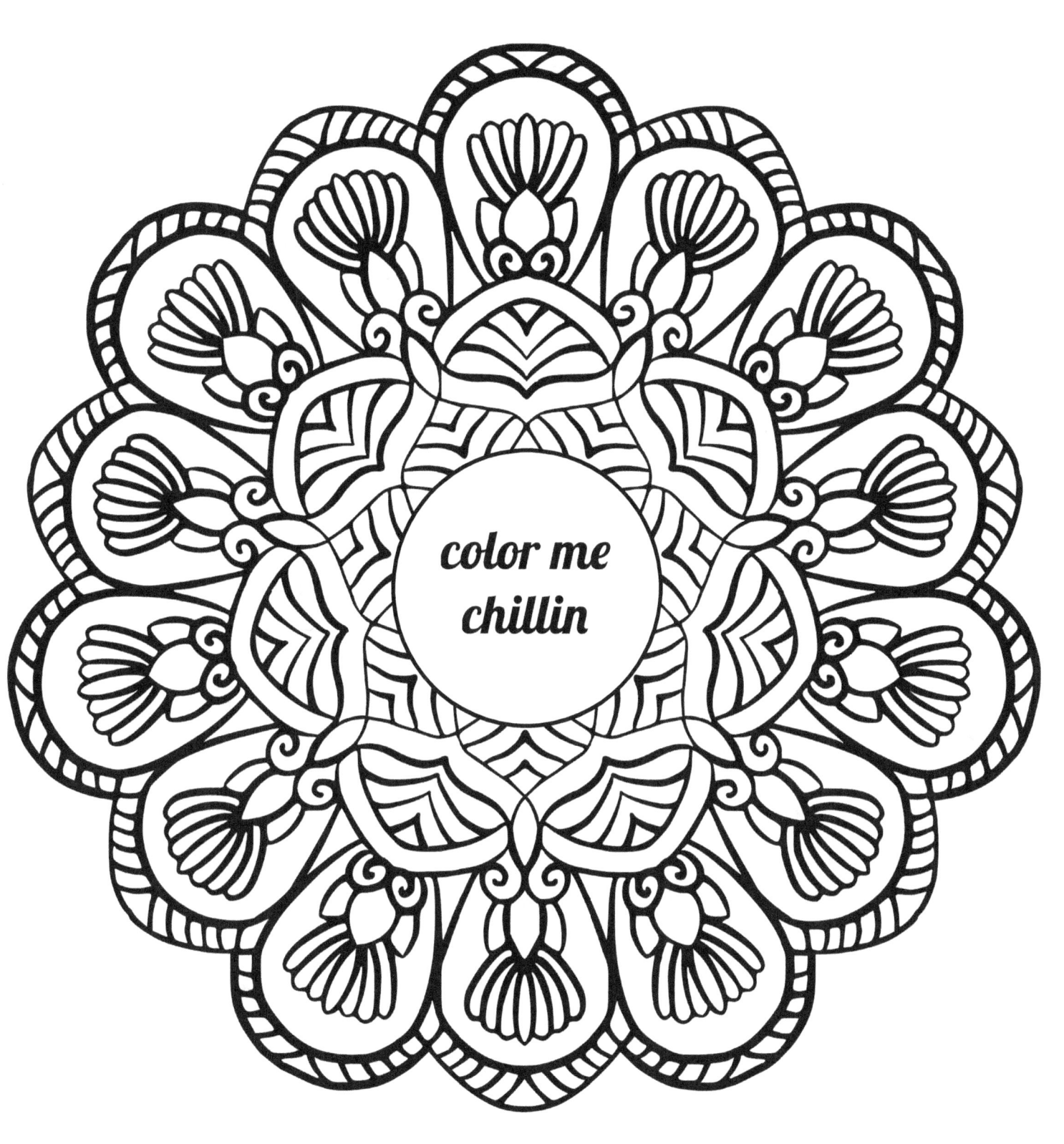

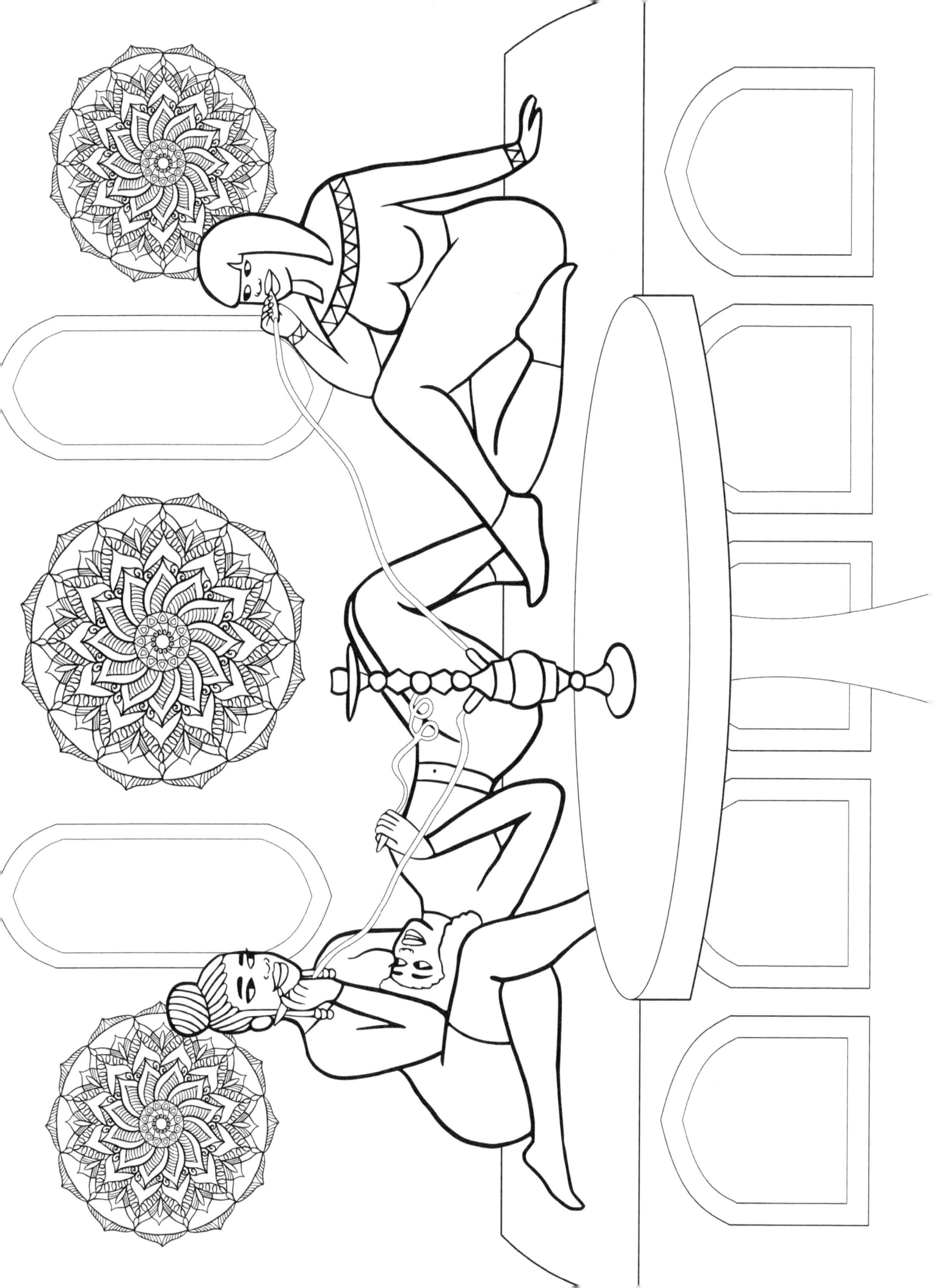

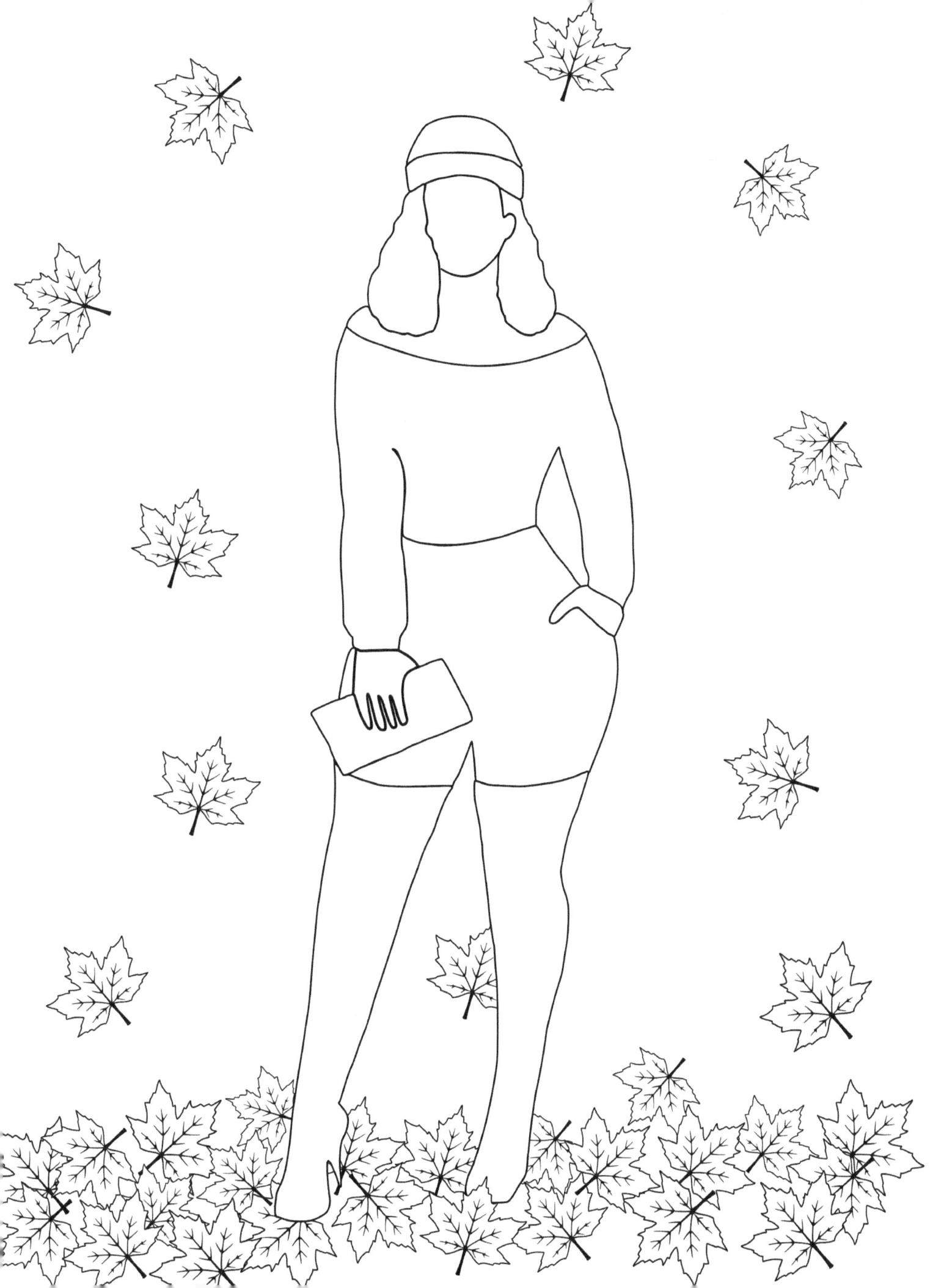

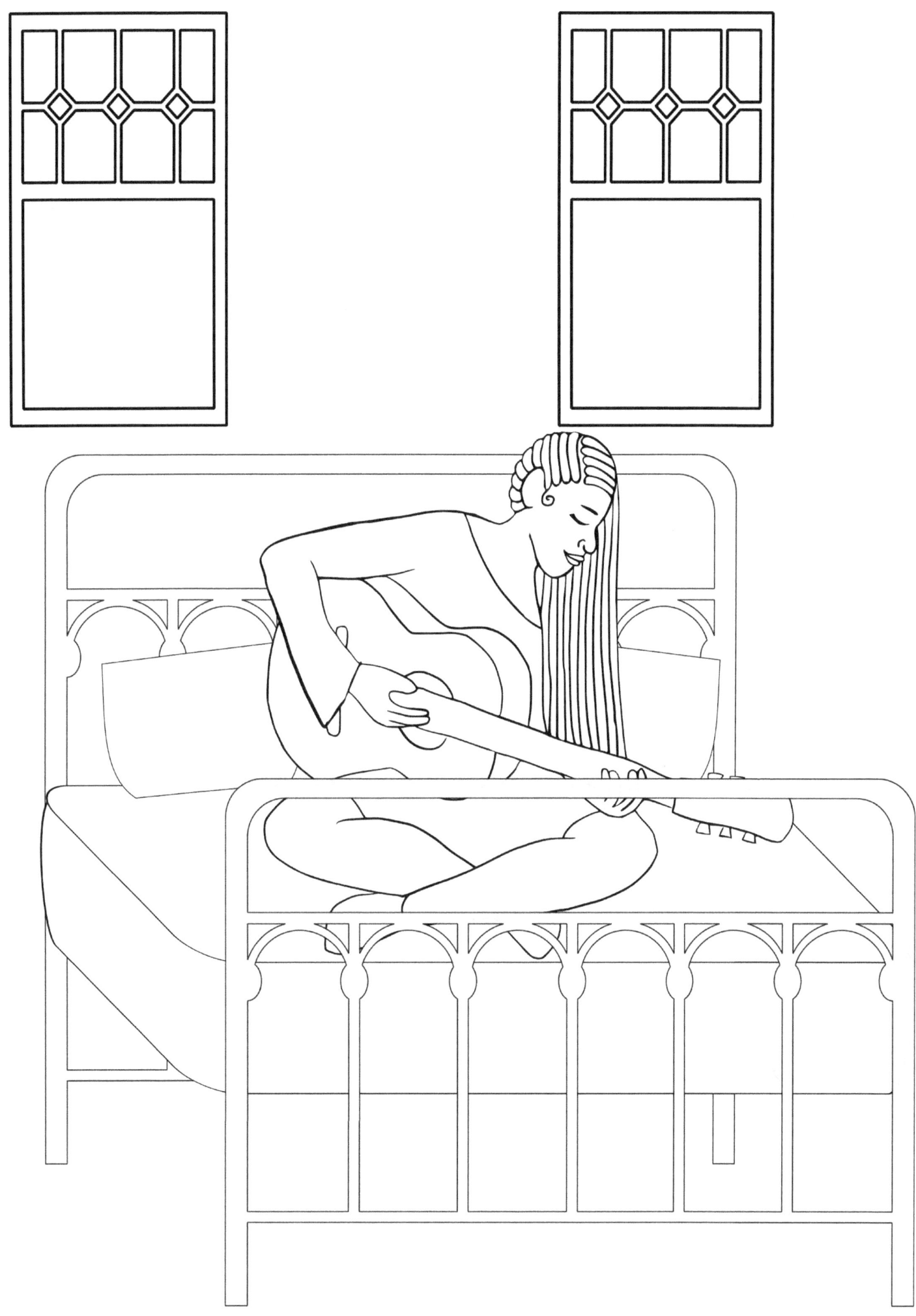

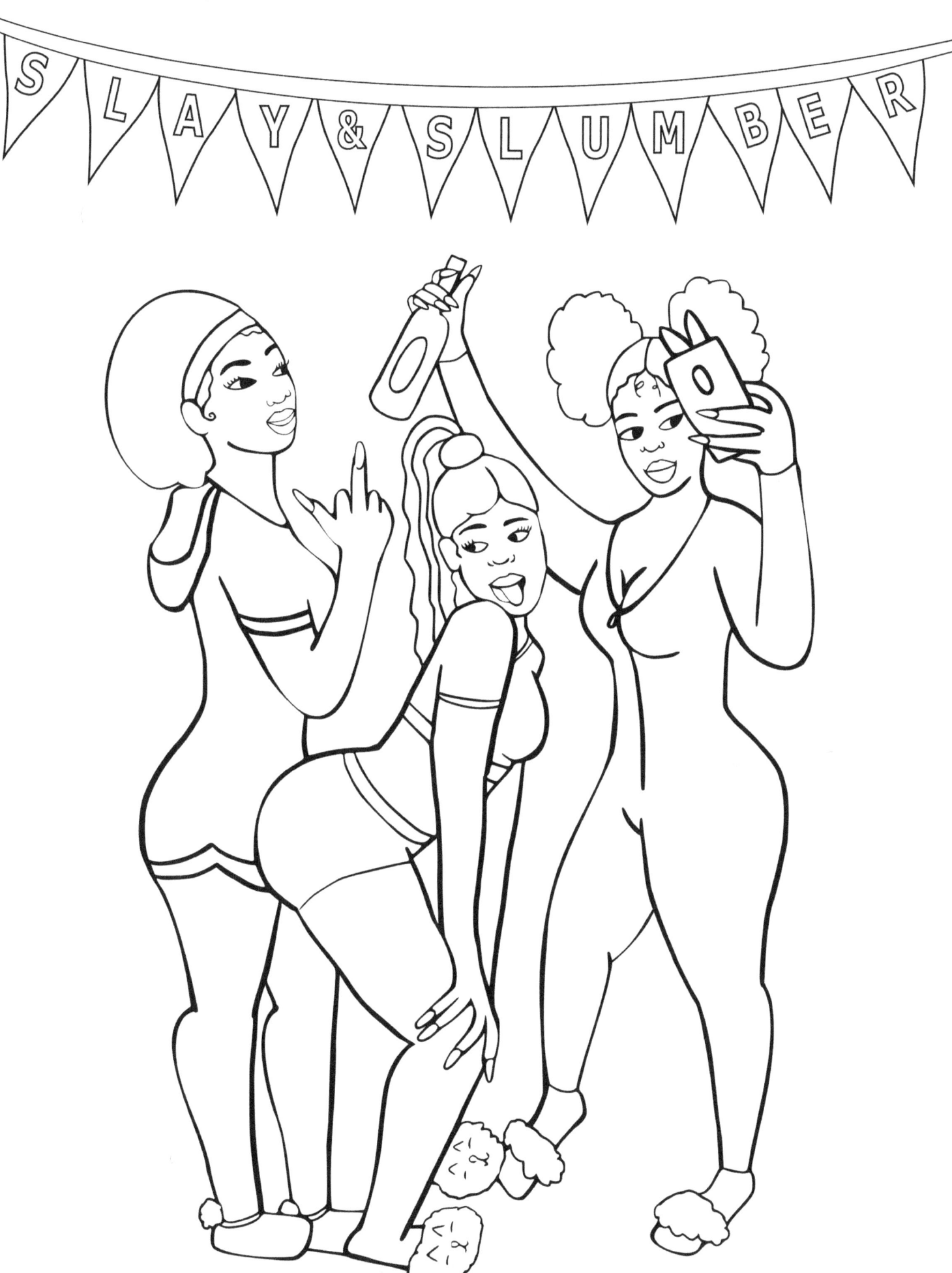

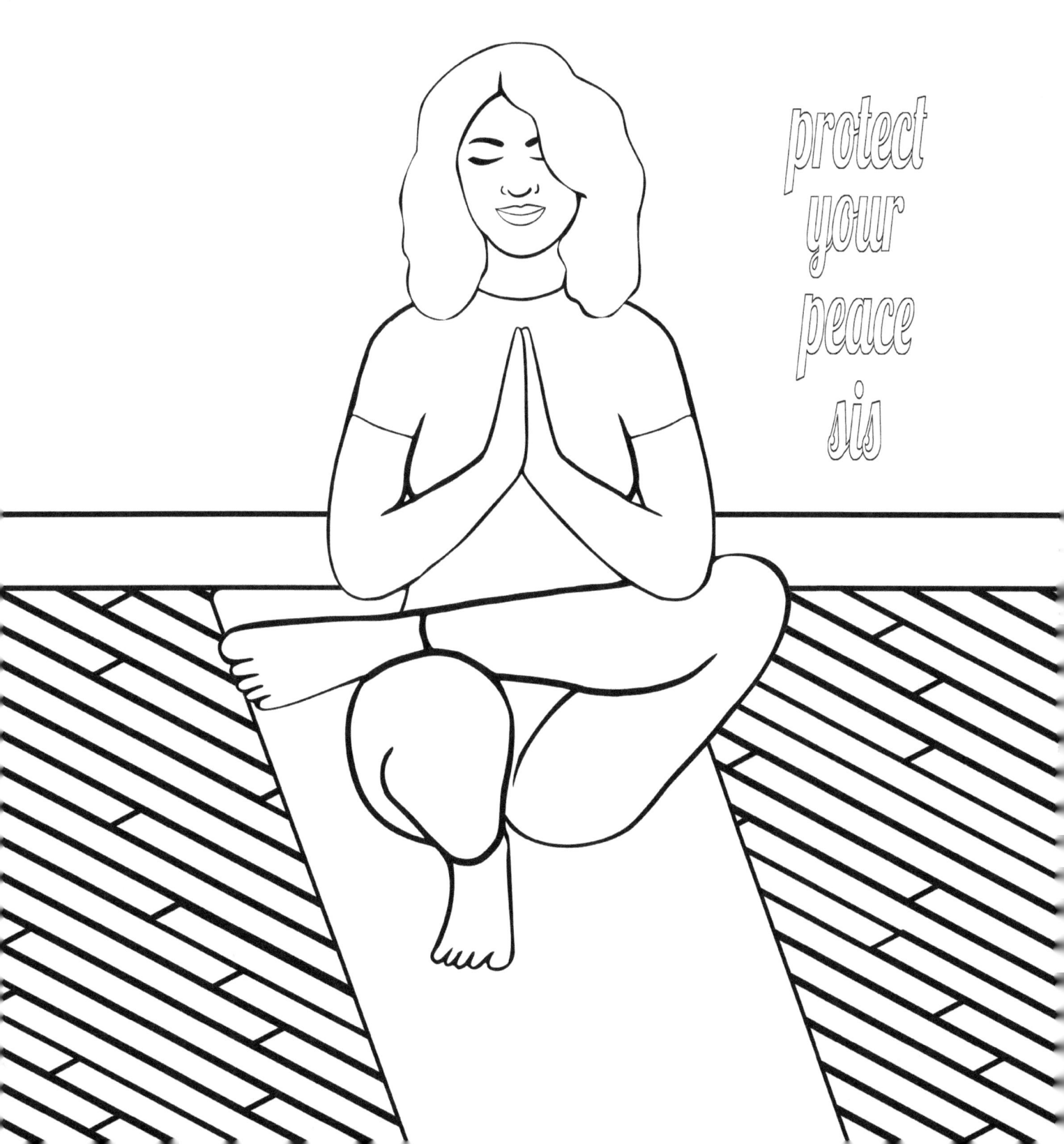

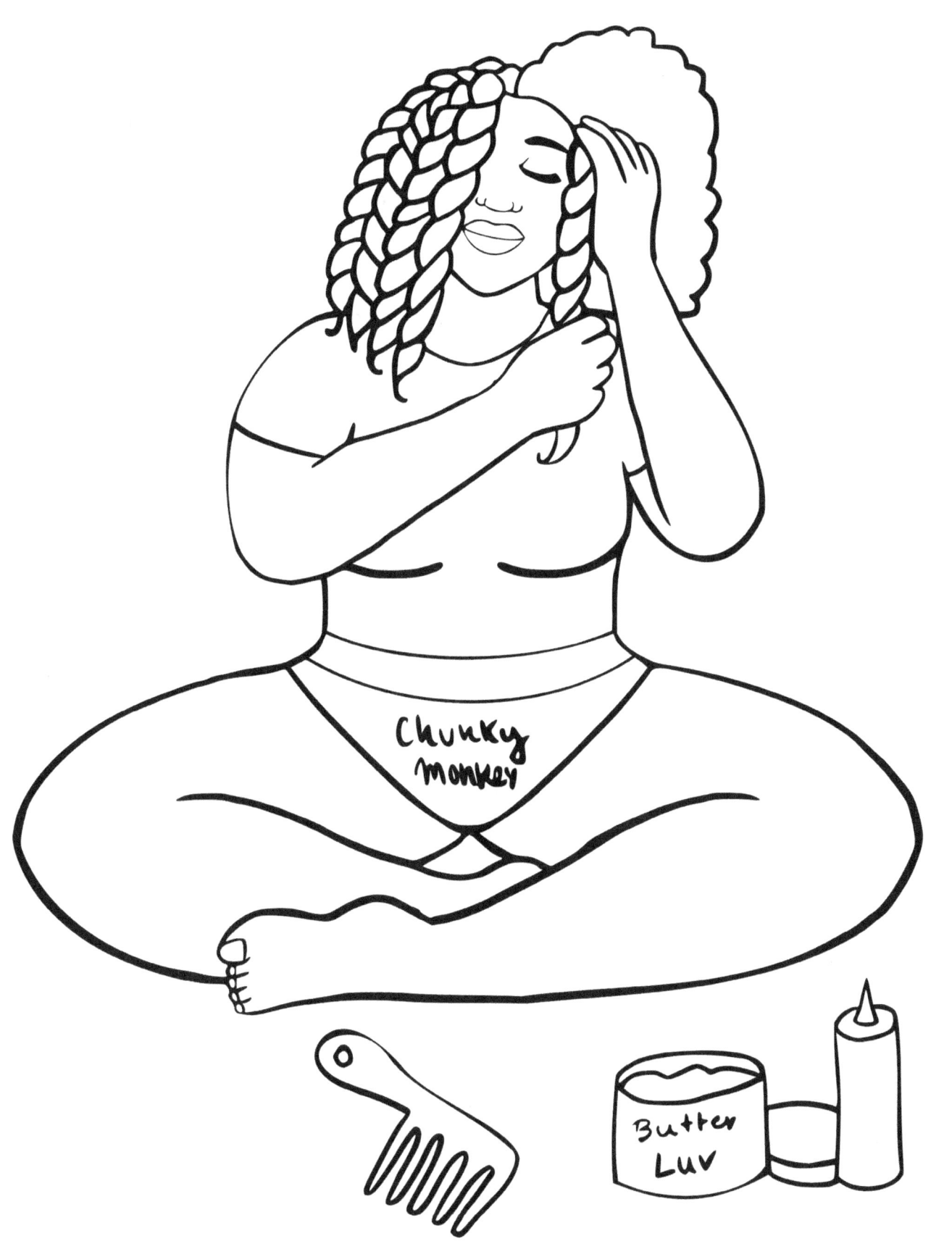

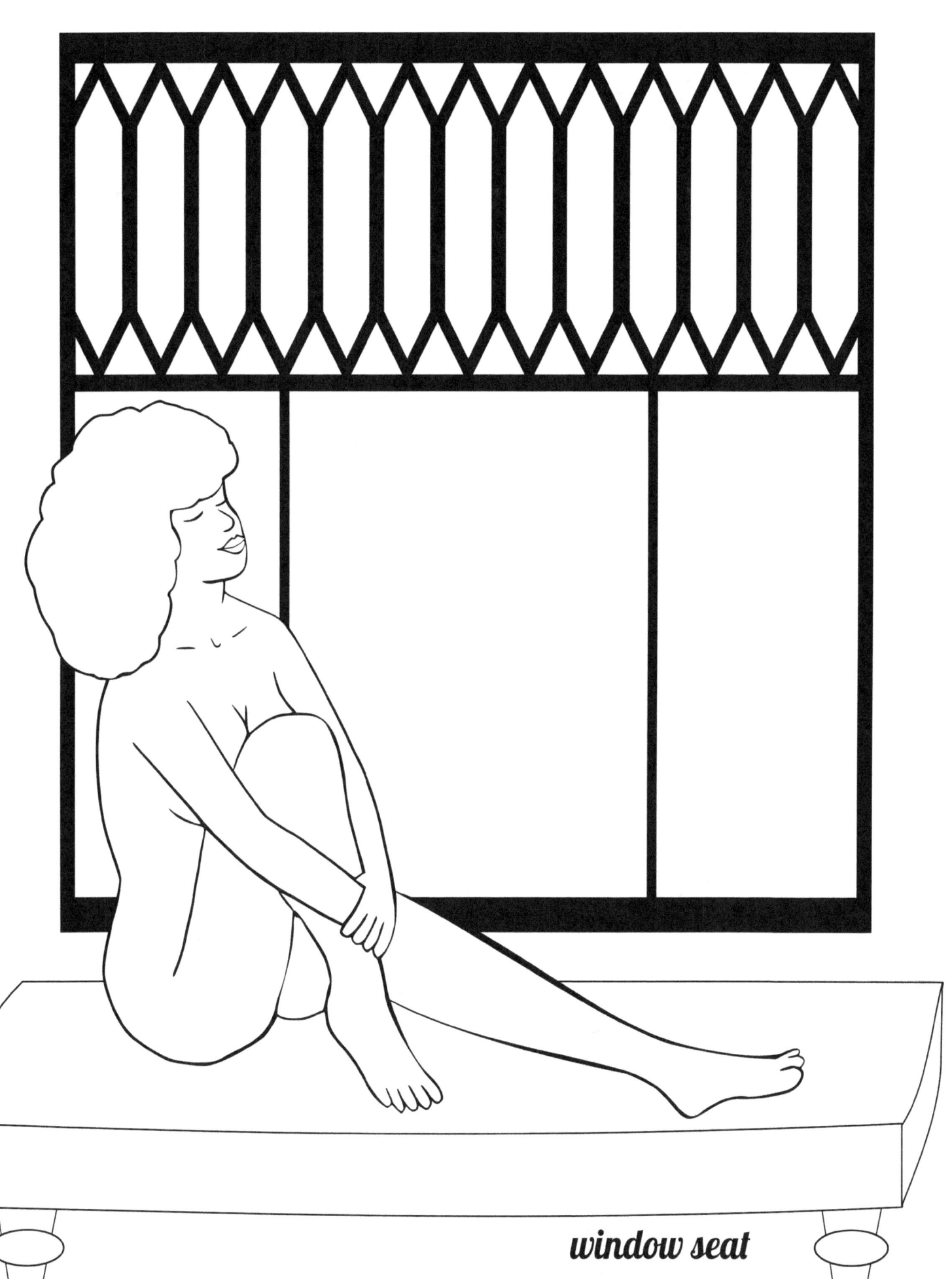

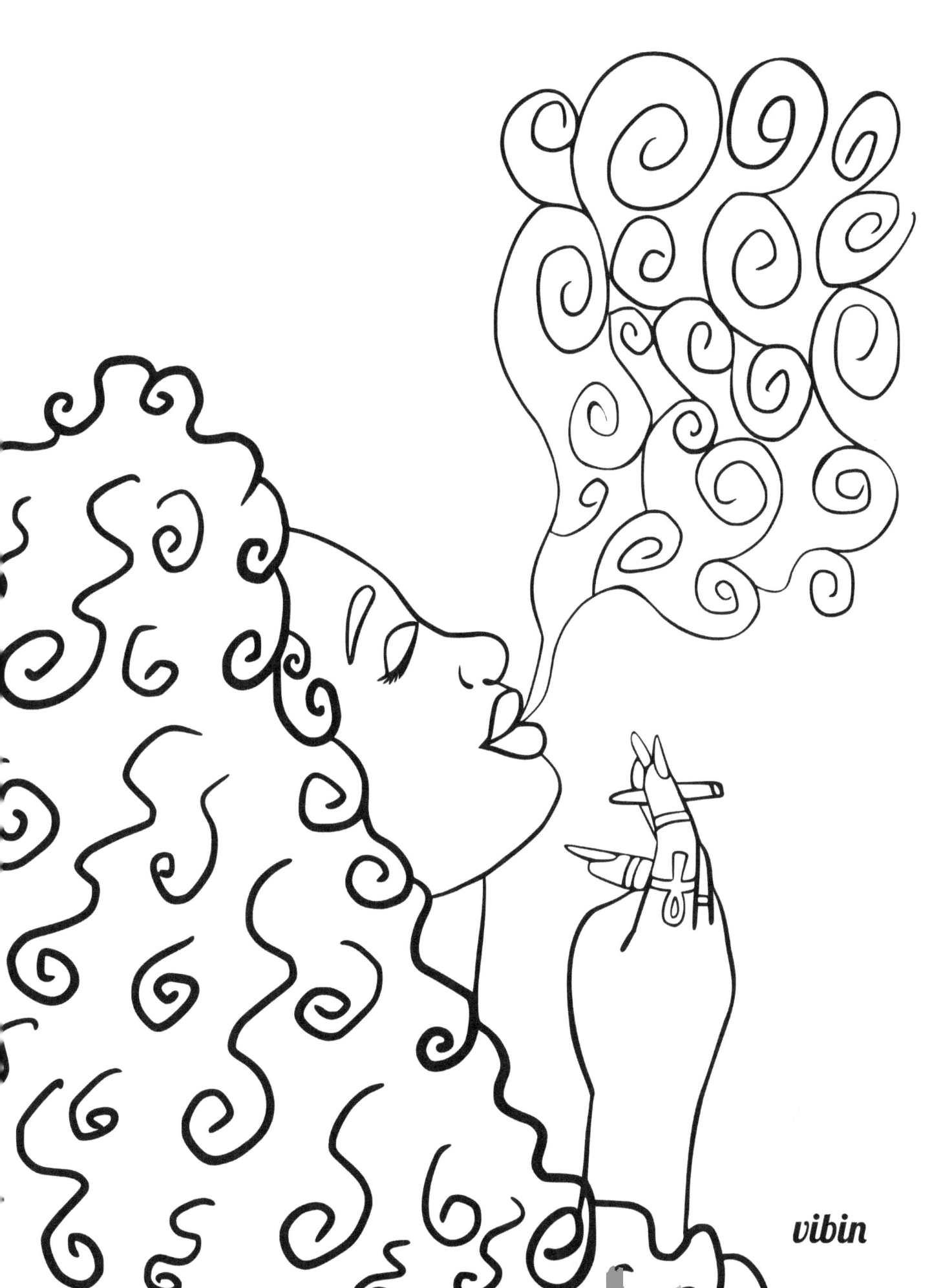

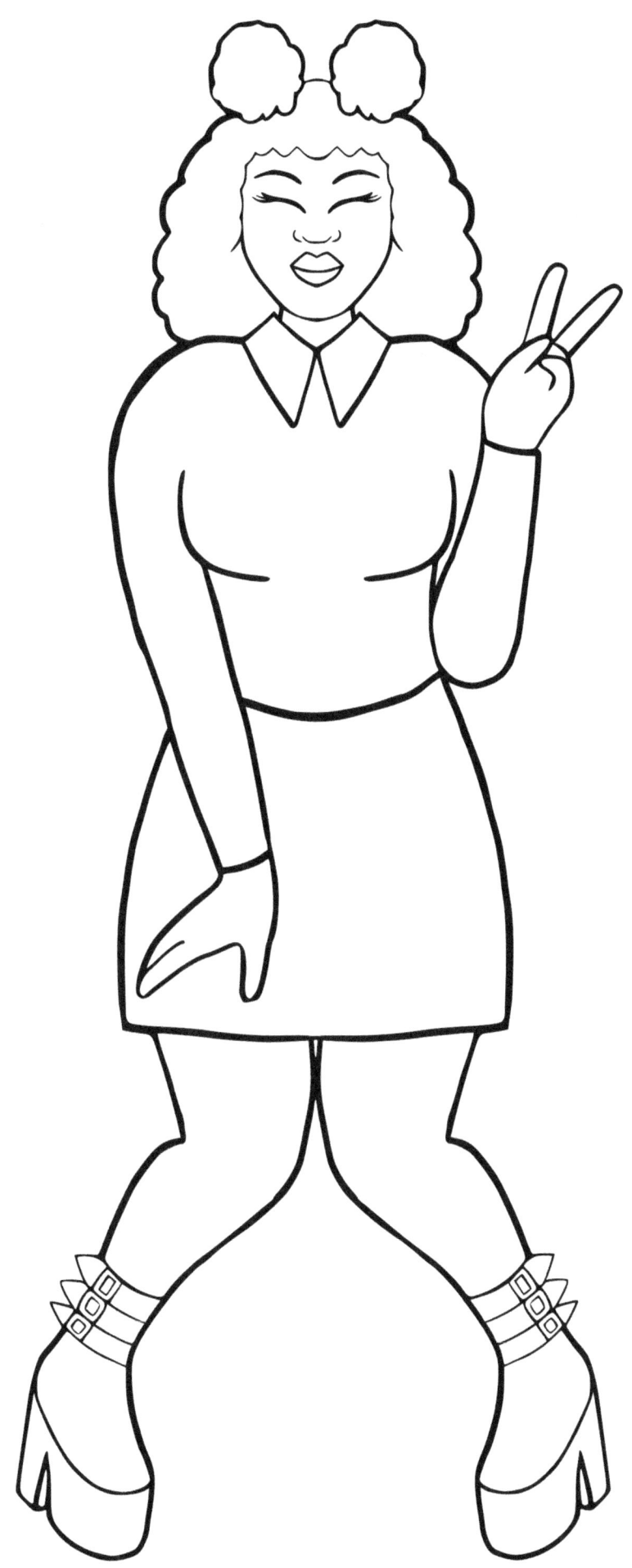

blaze n bathe

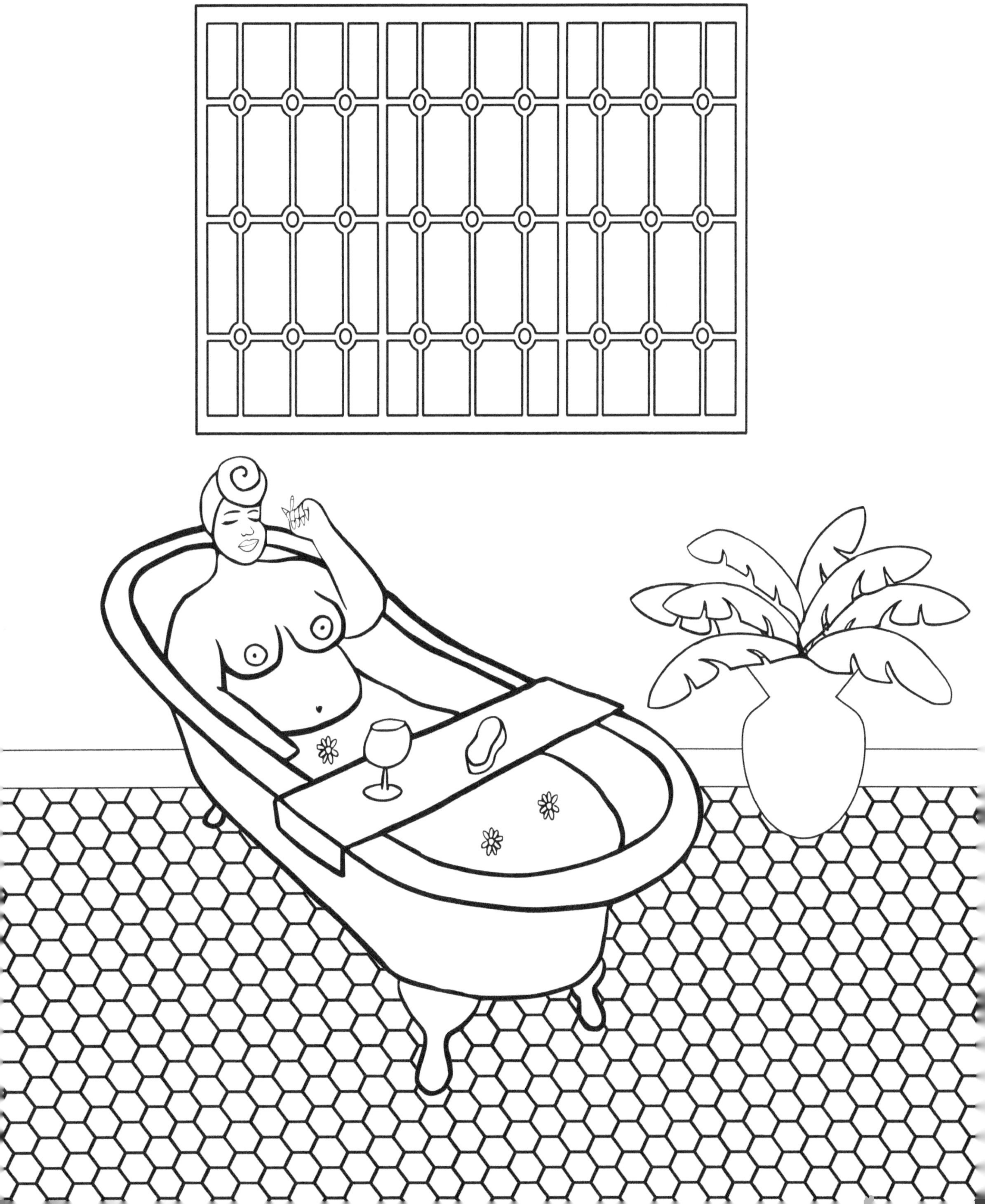

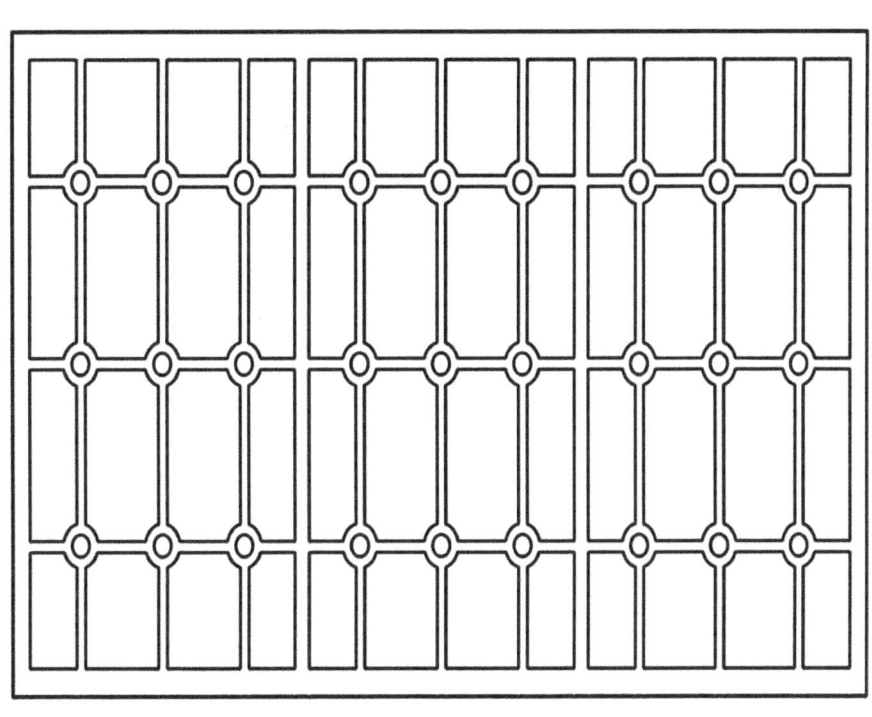

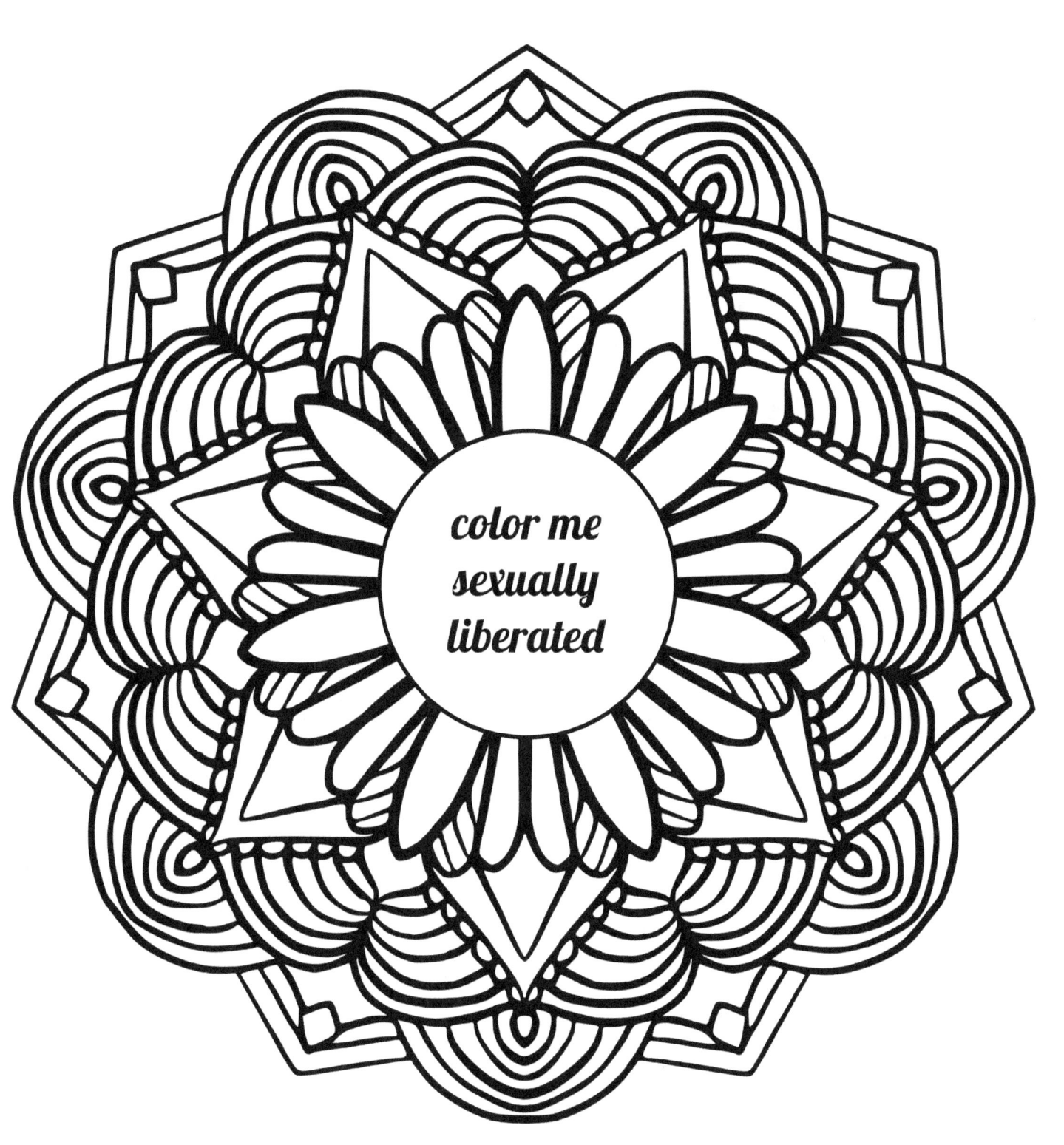

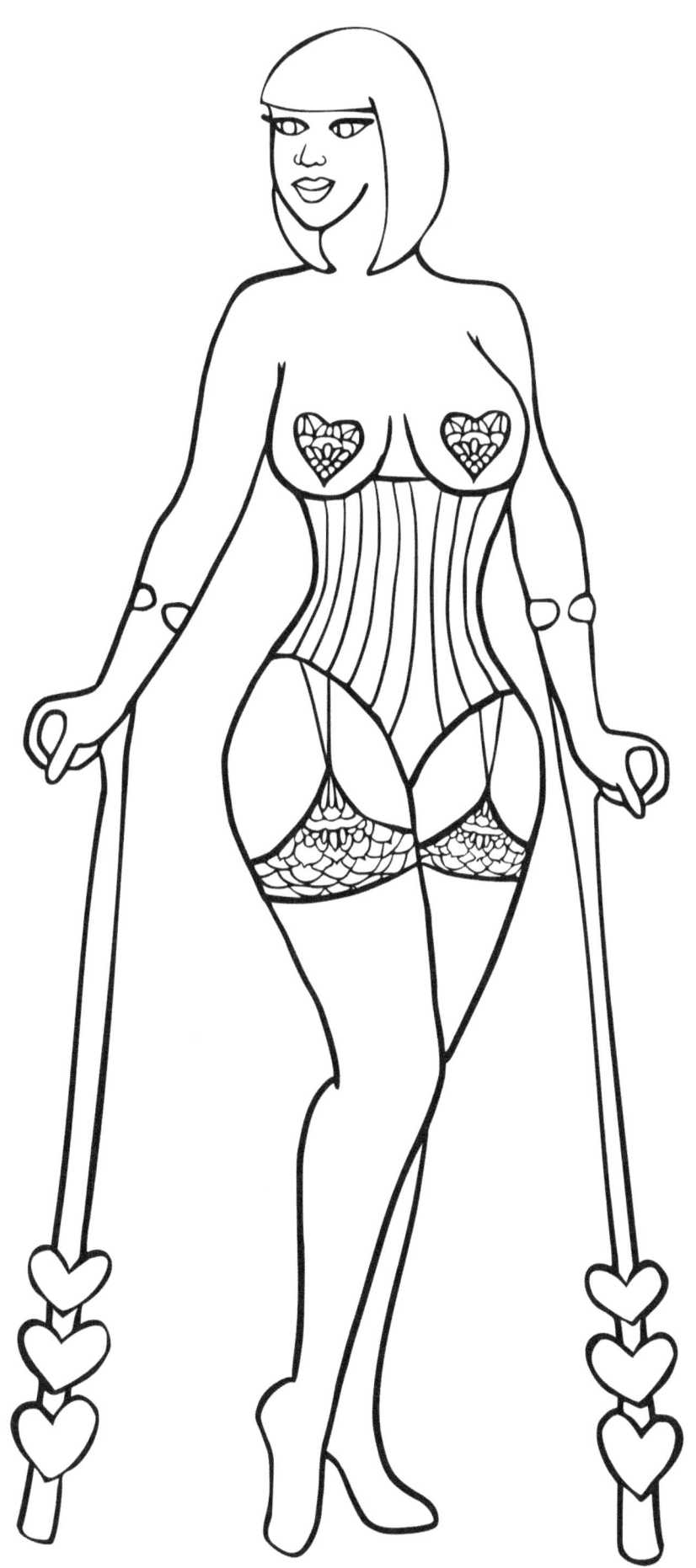

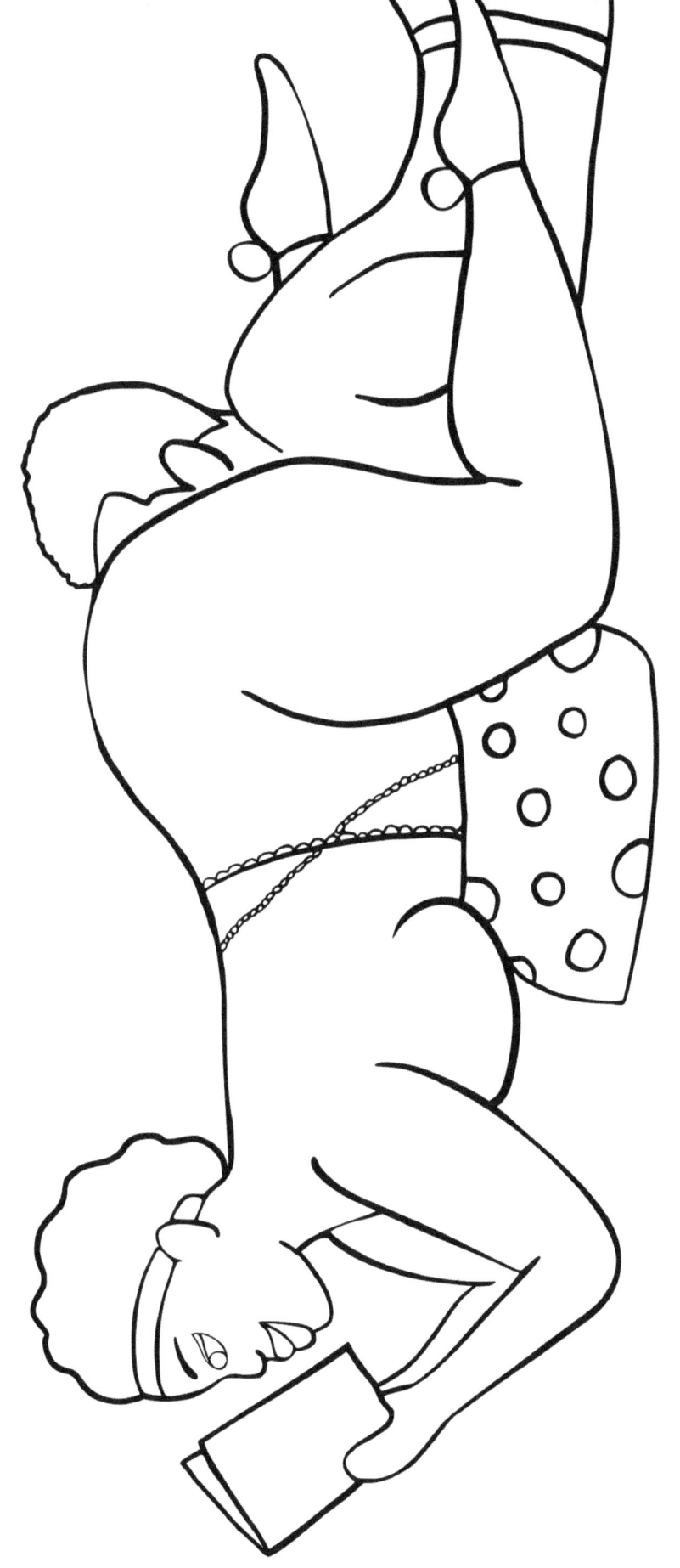

snack time

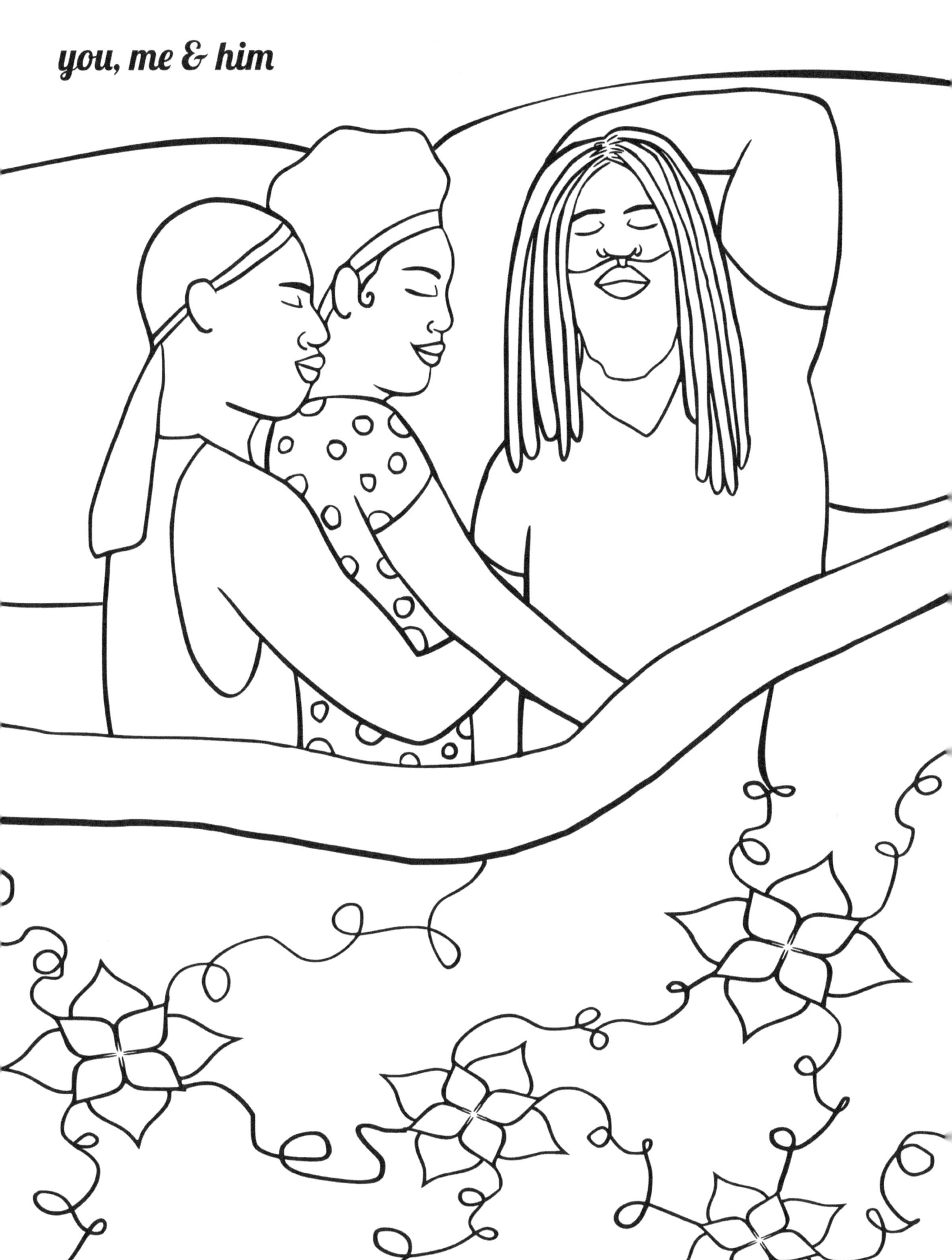

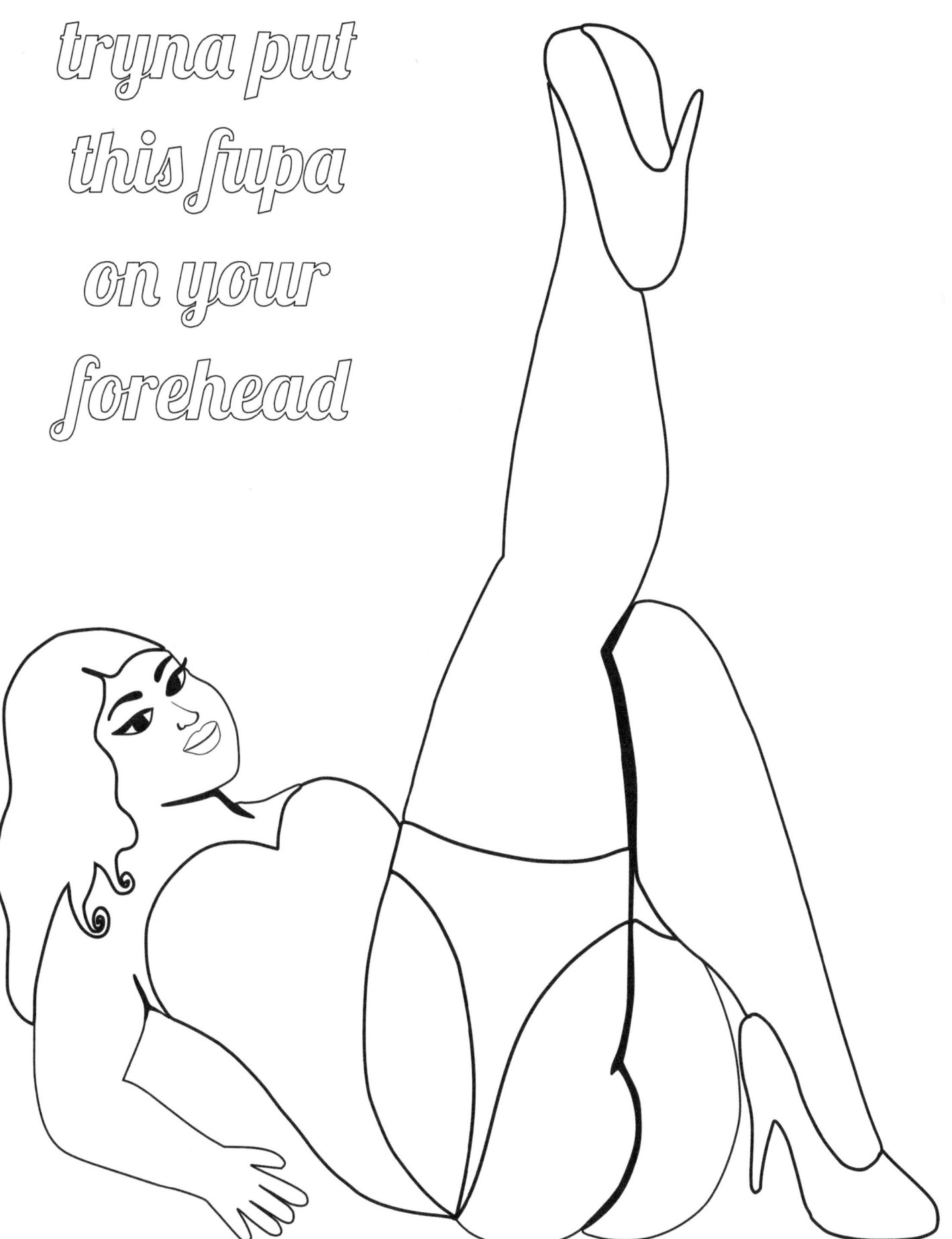

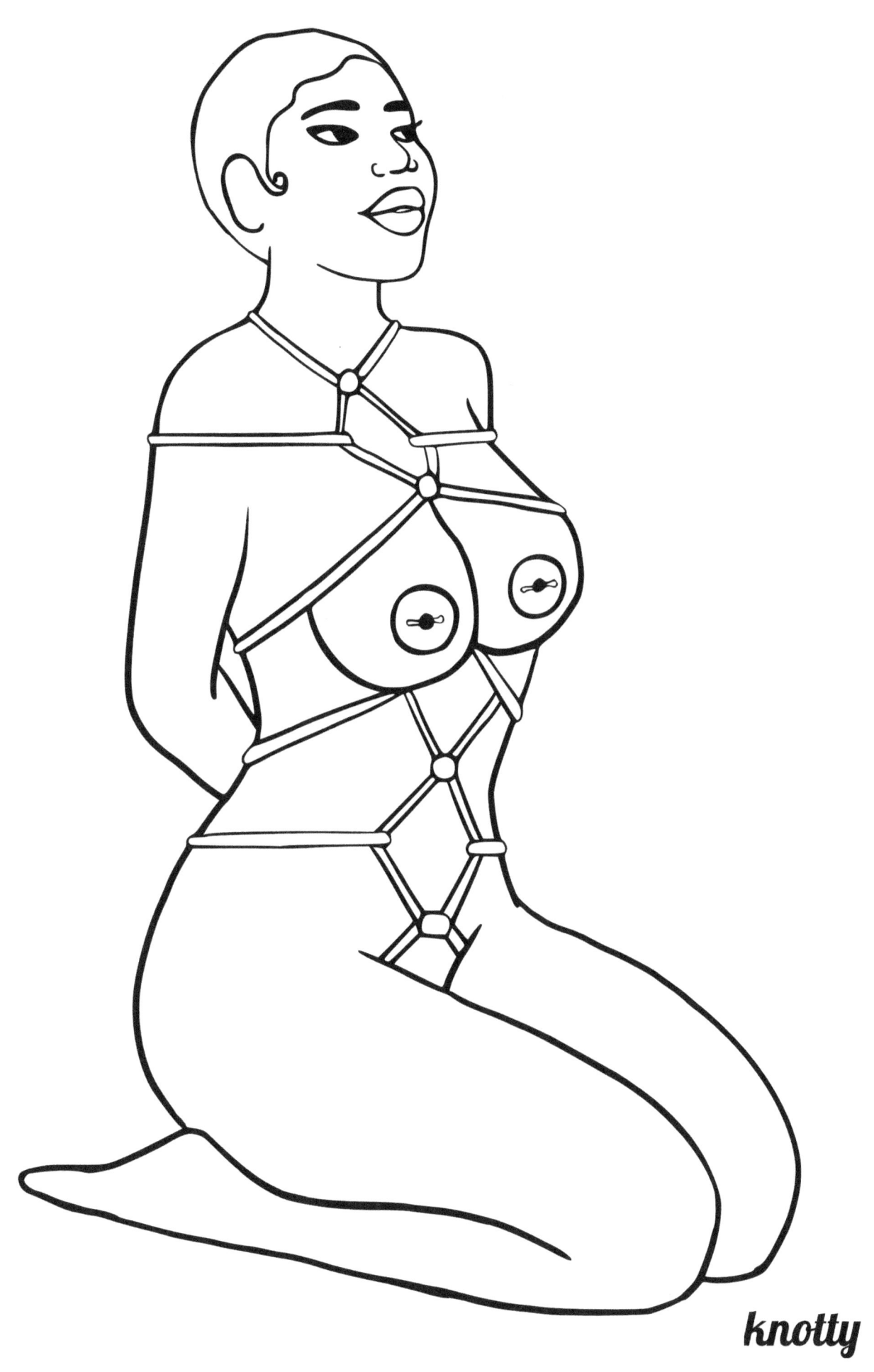

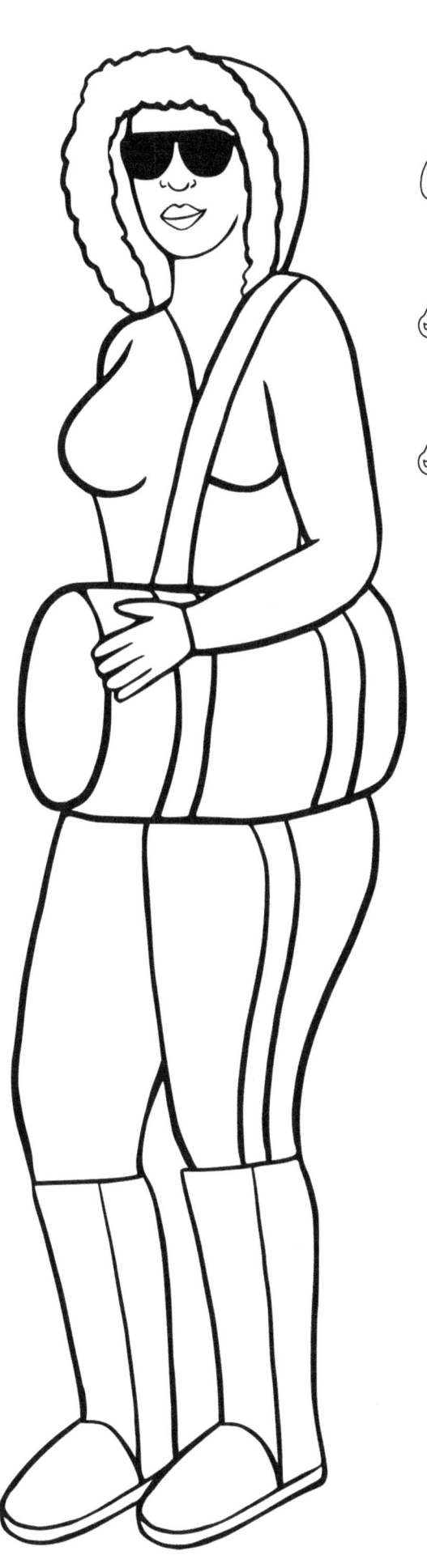

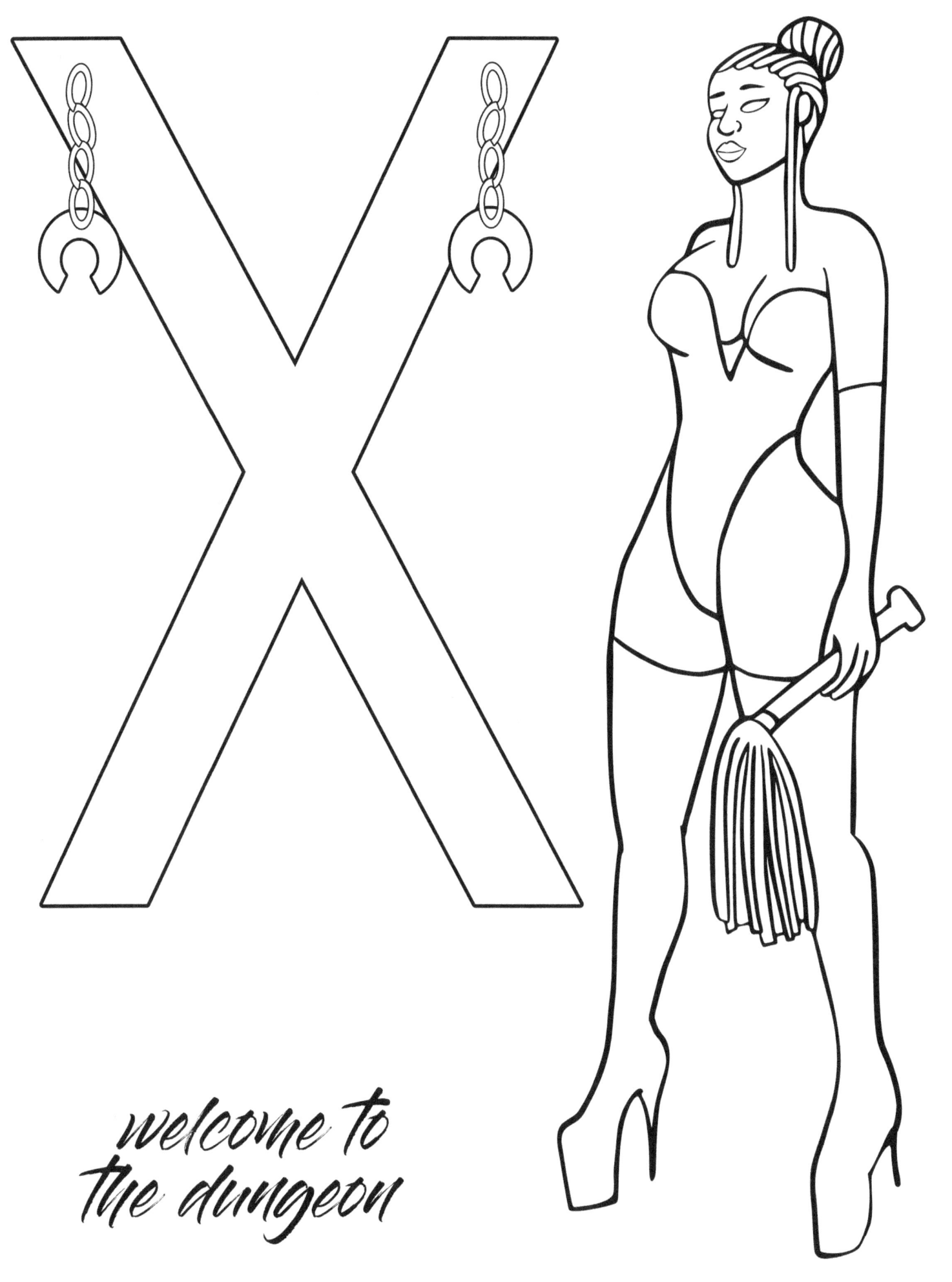

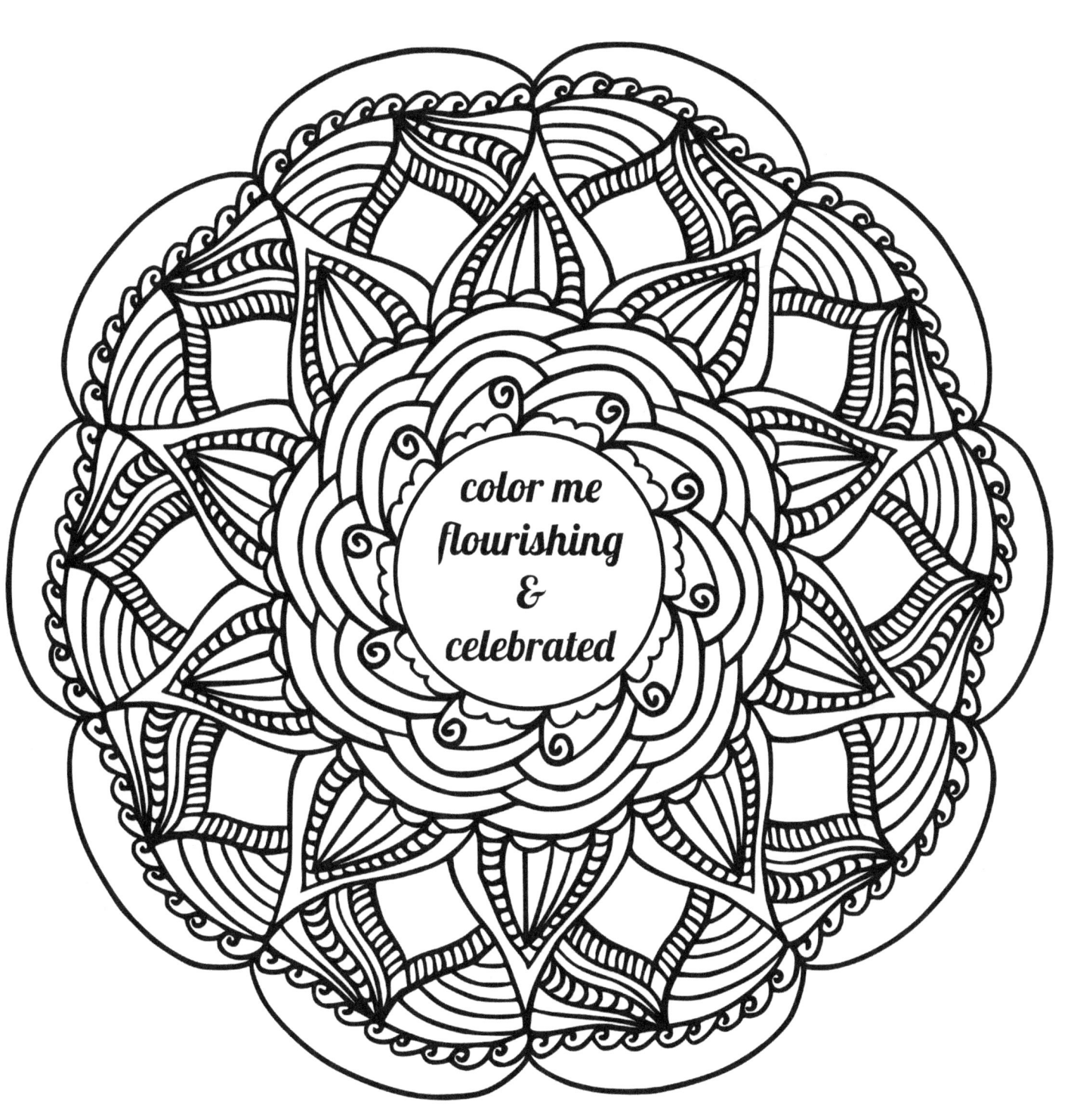

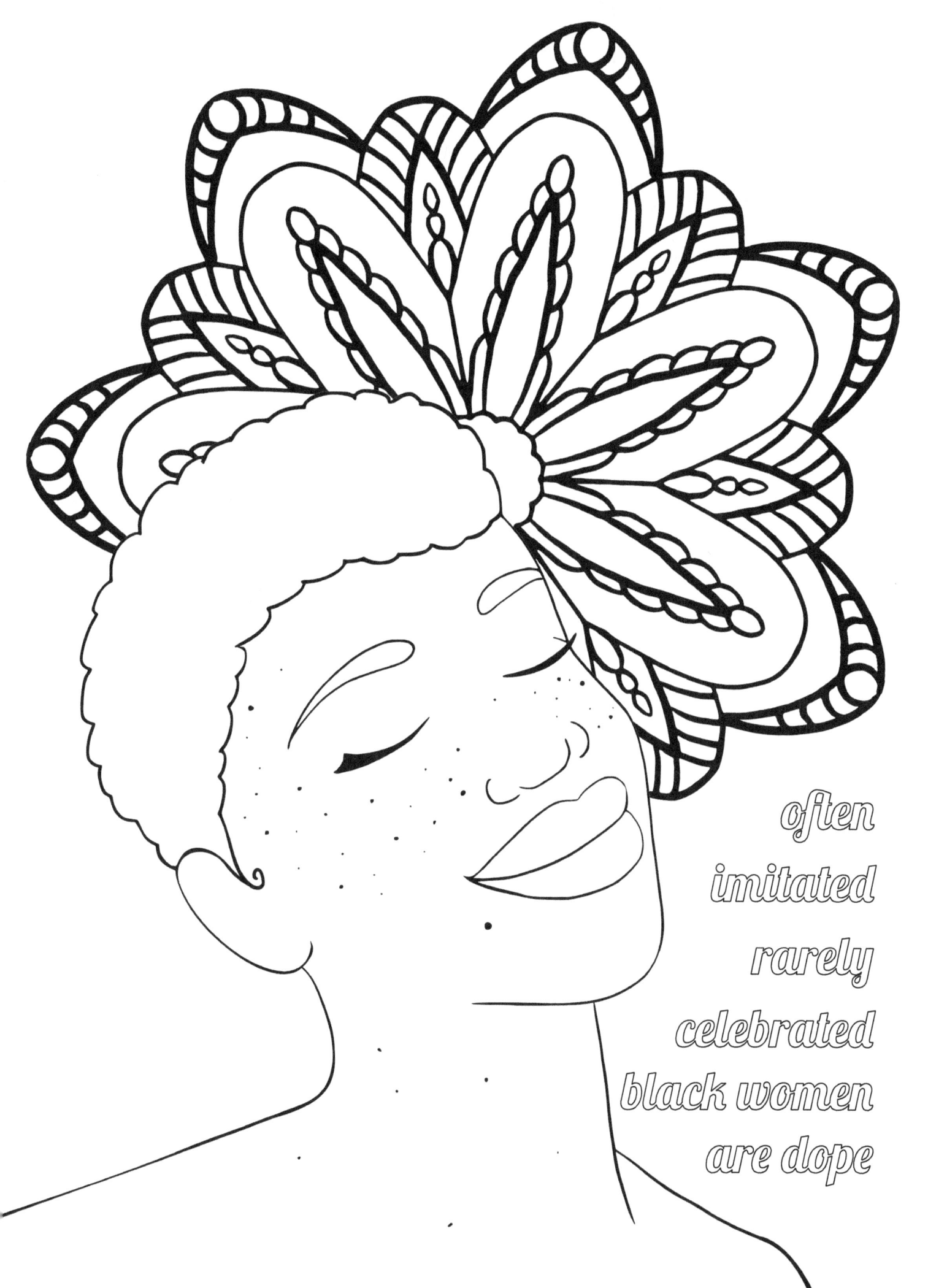

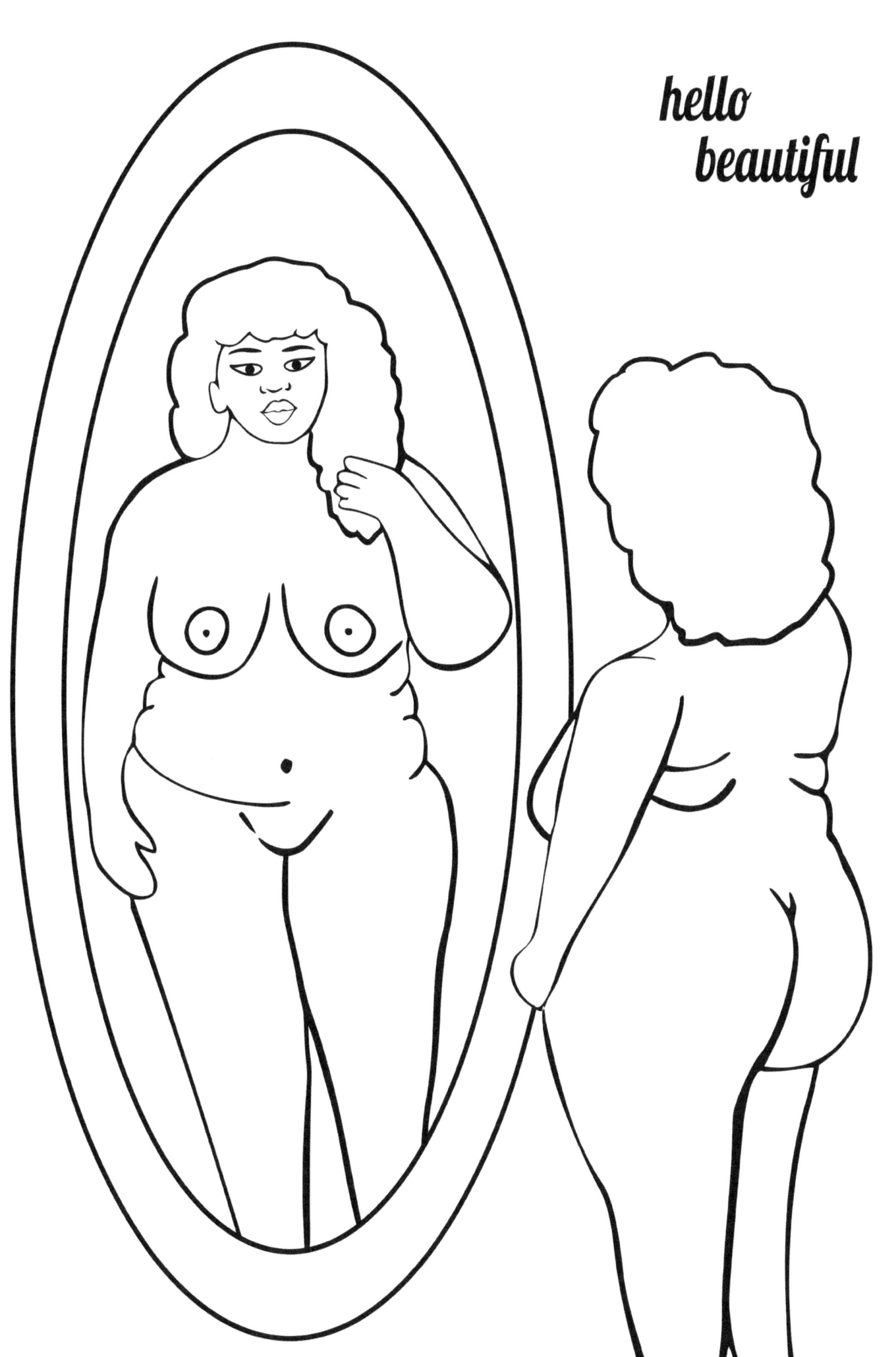

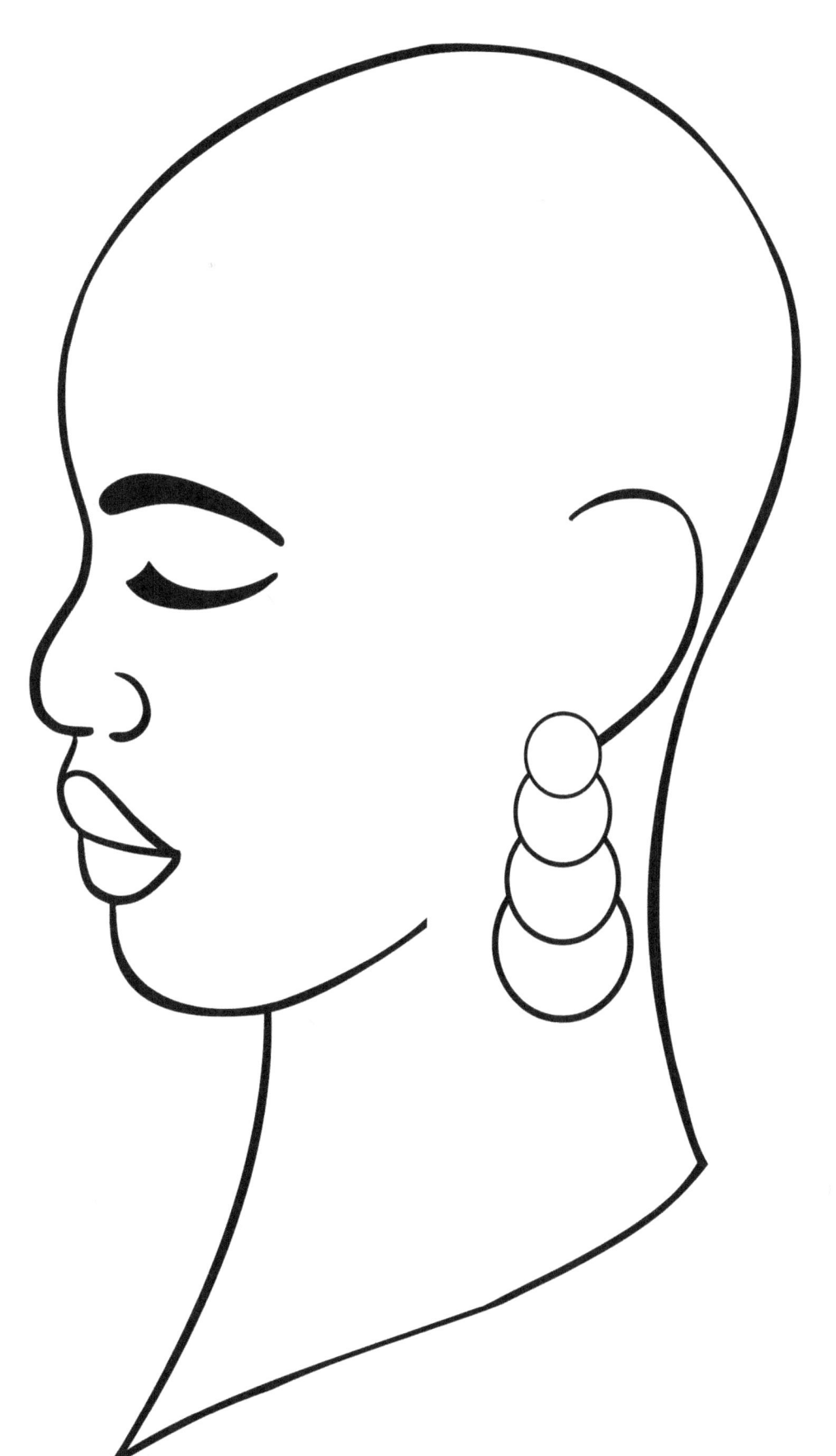

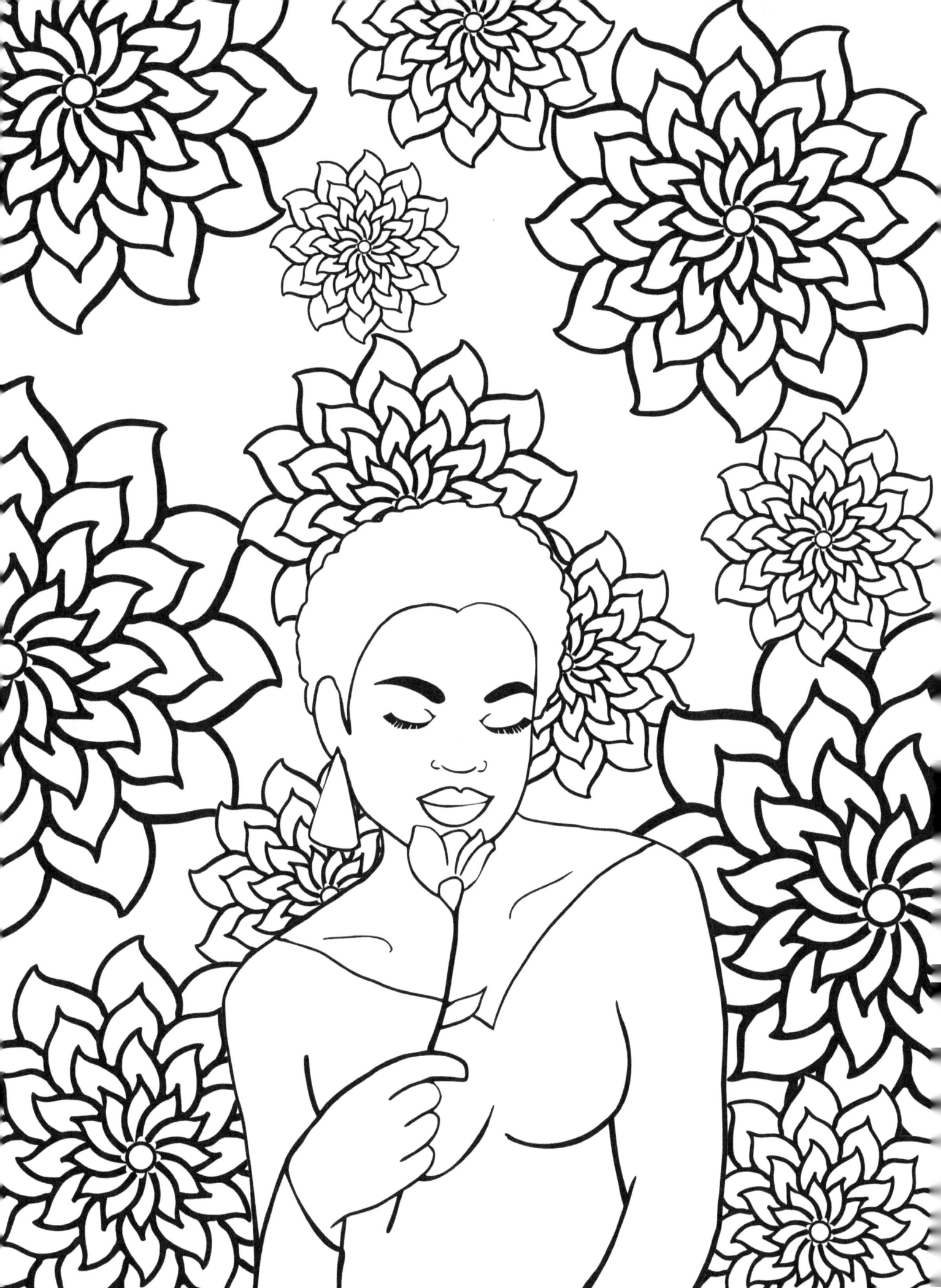

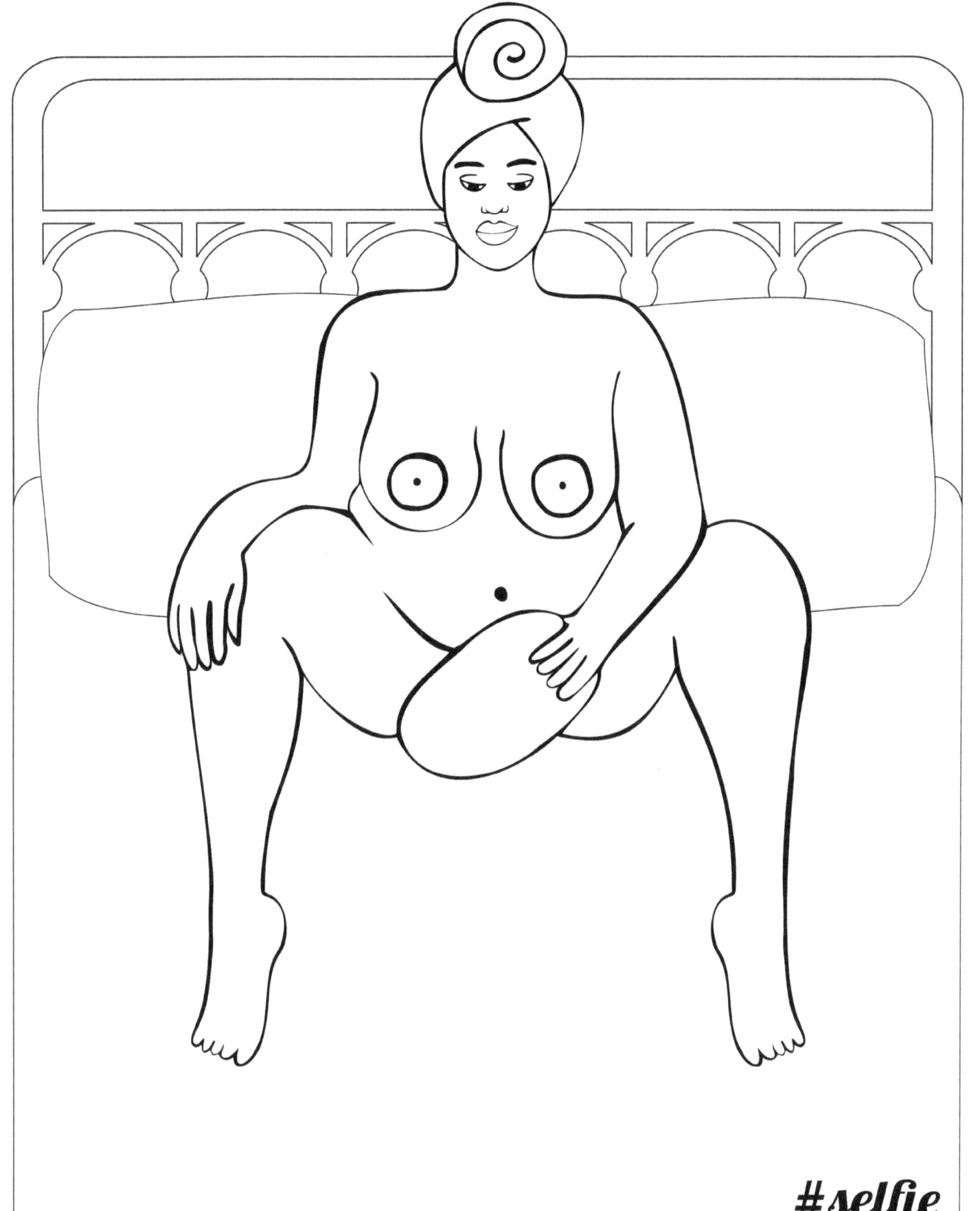

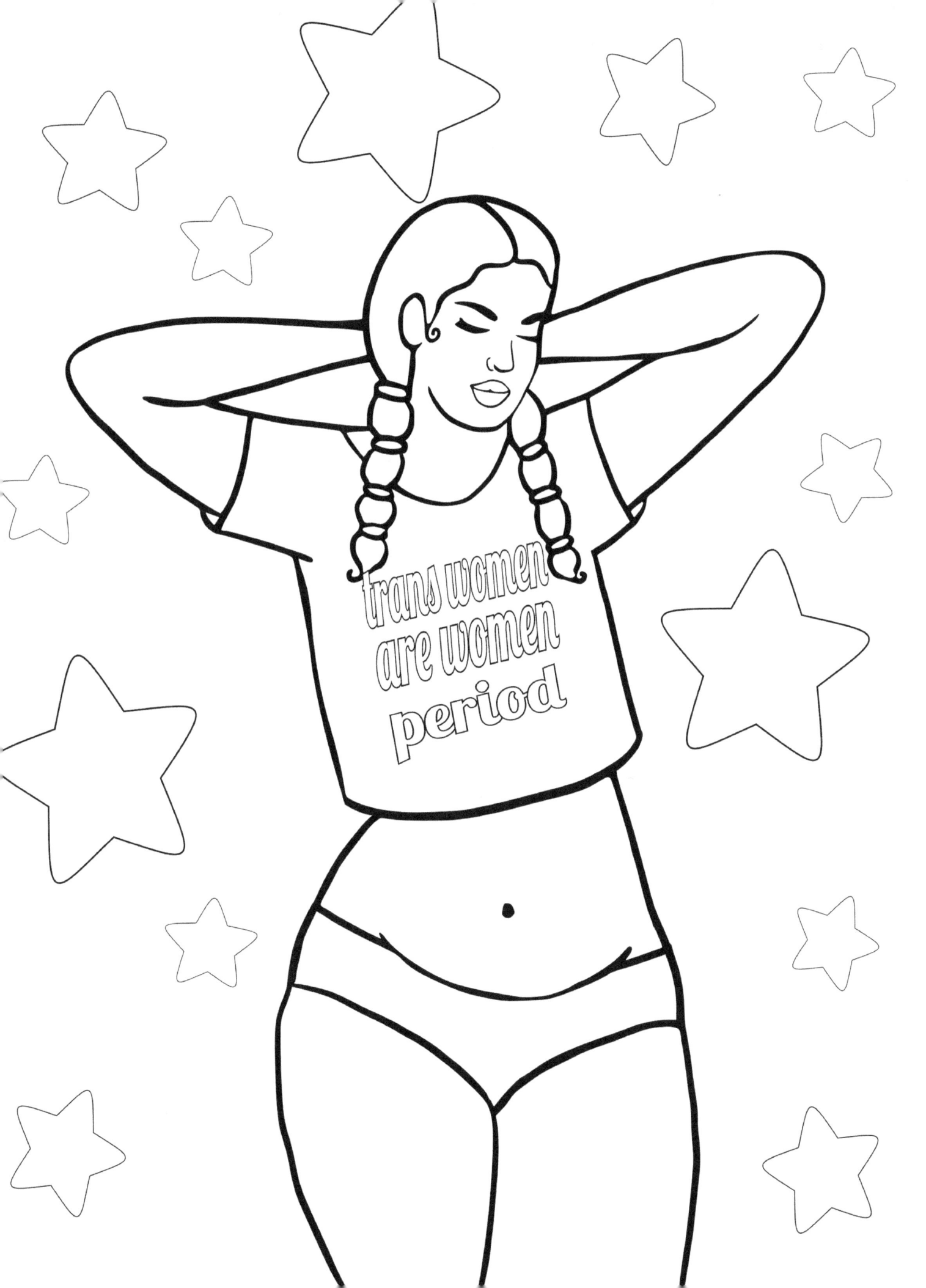

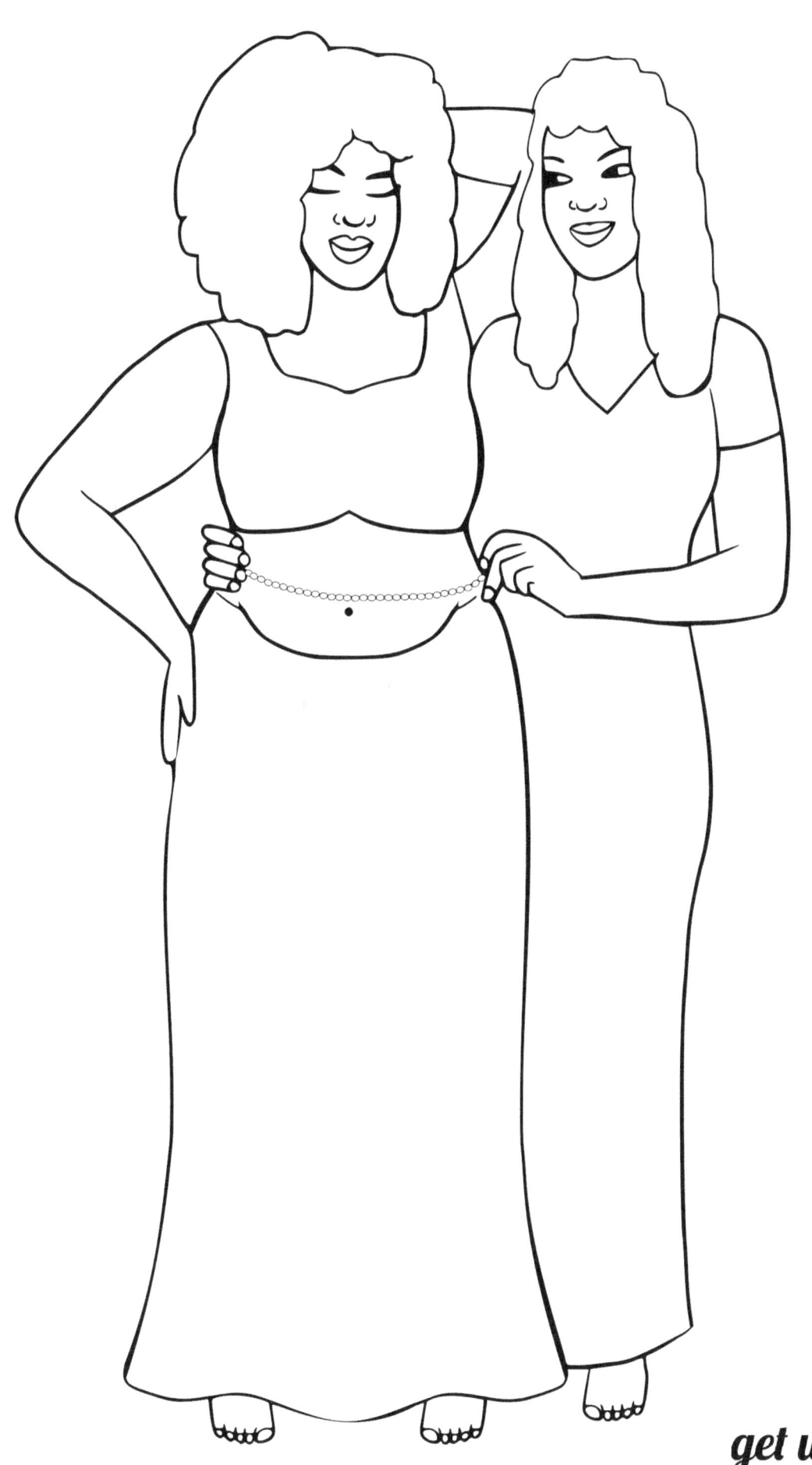

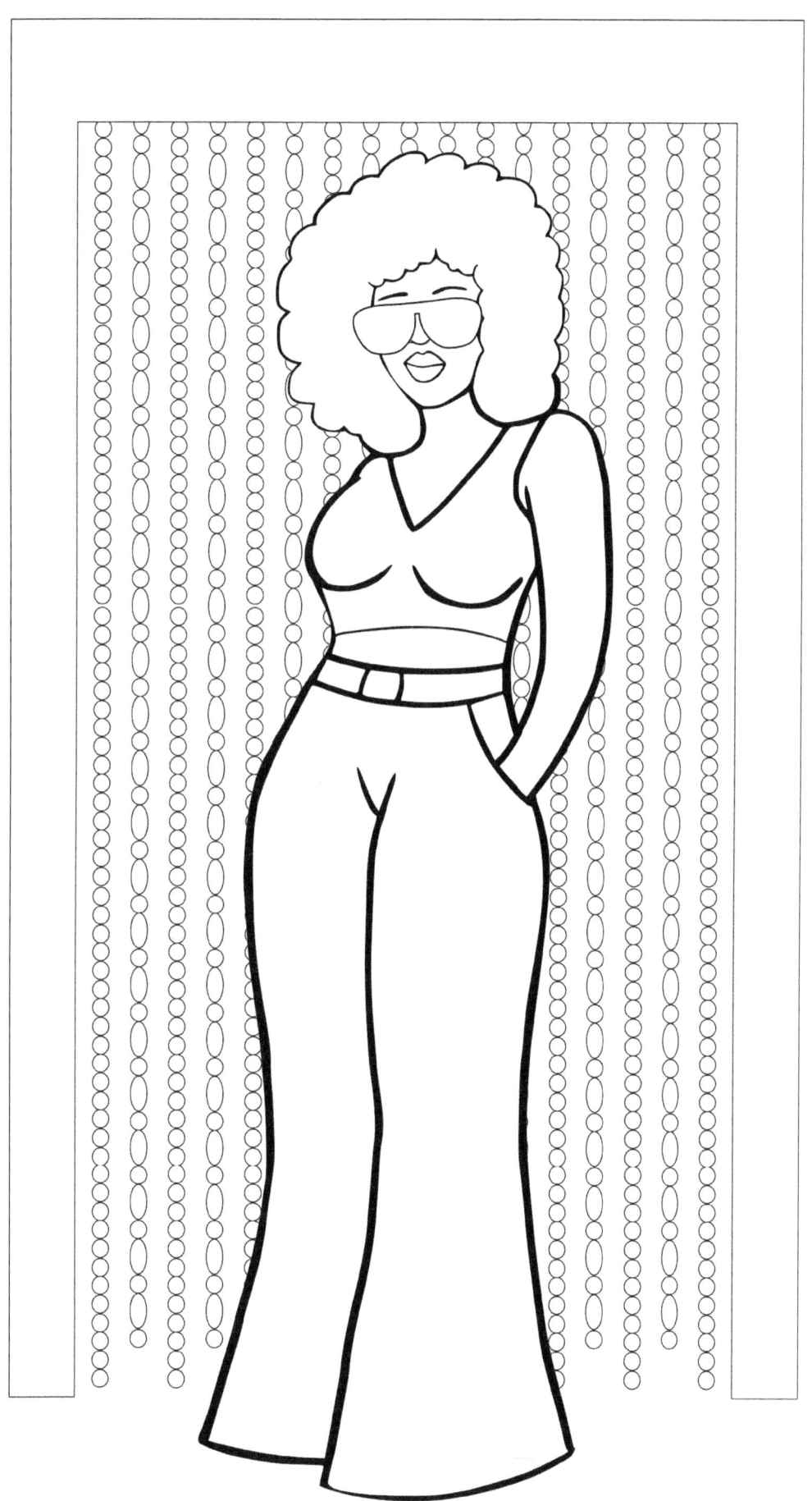

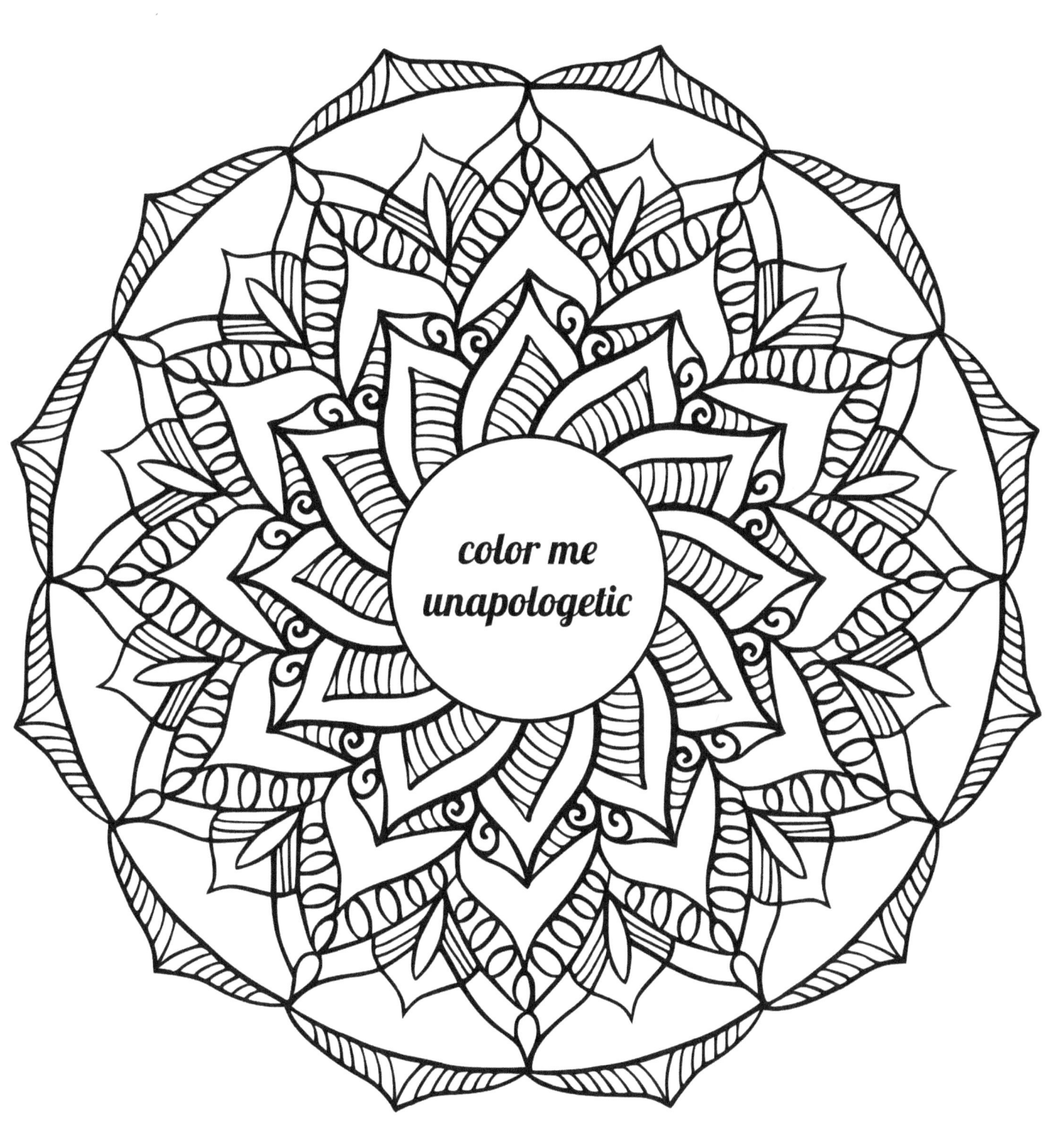

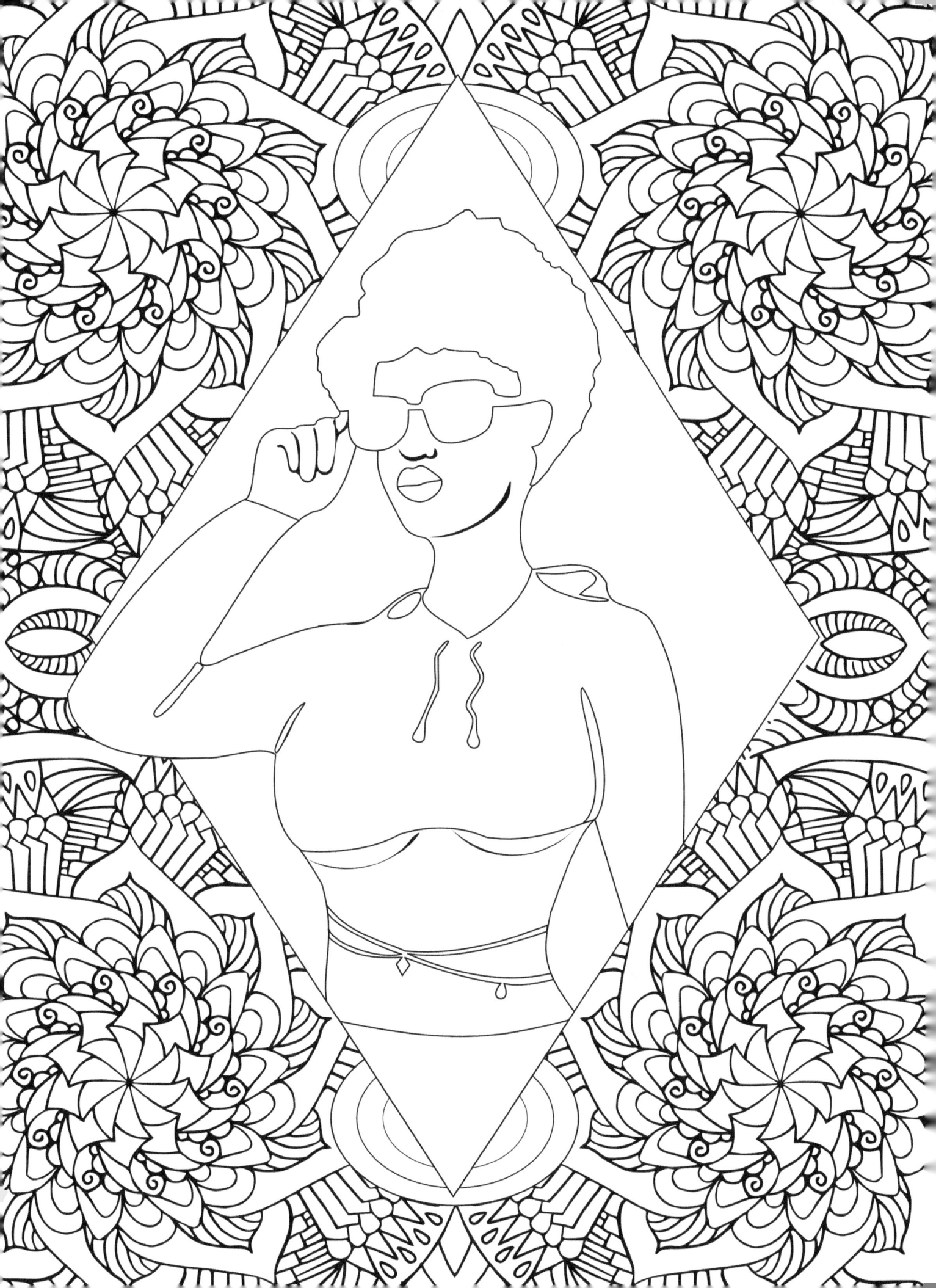

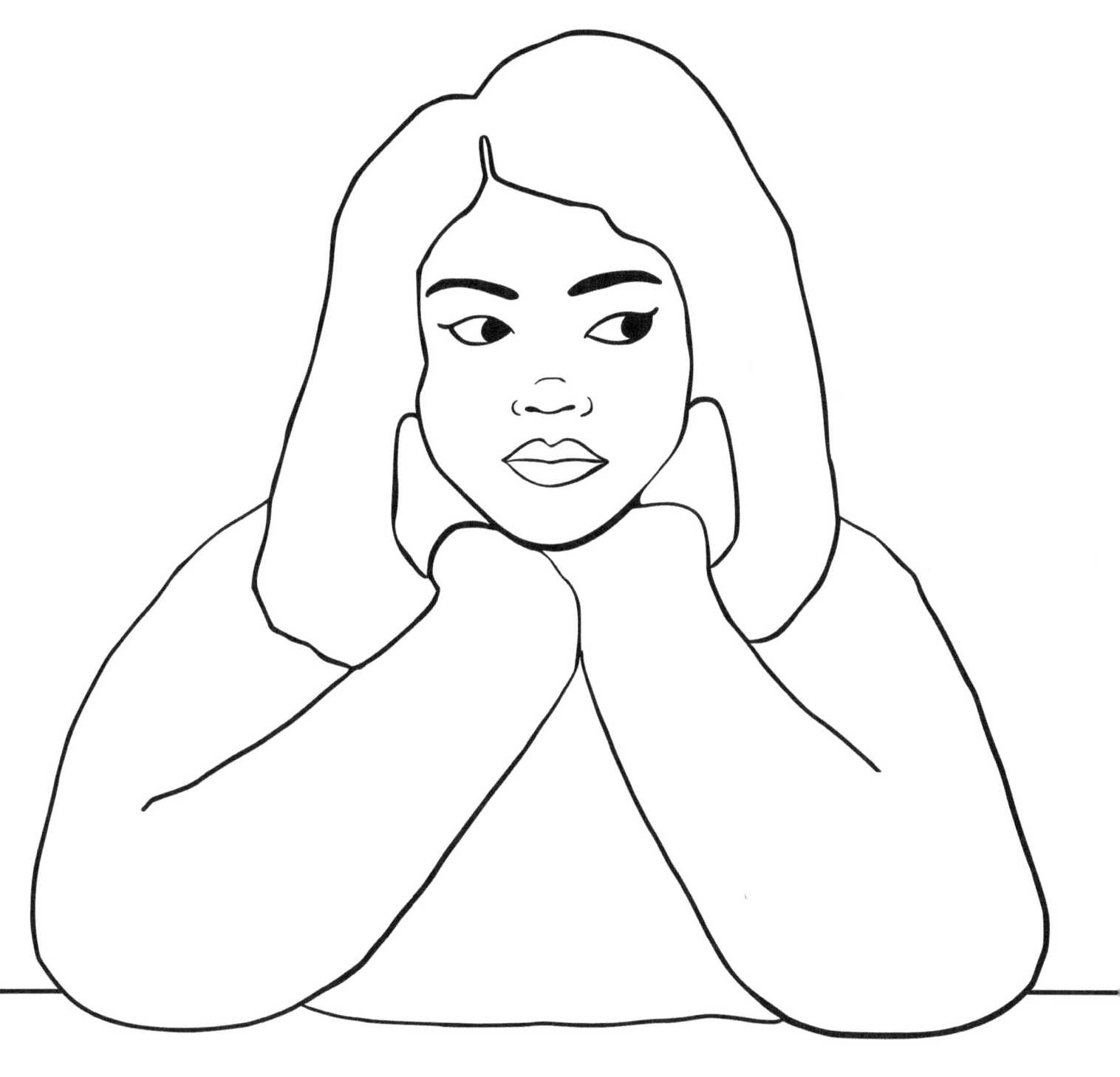

peepin shit

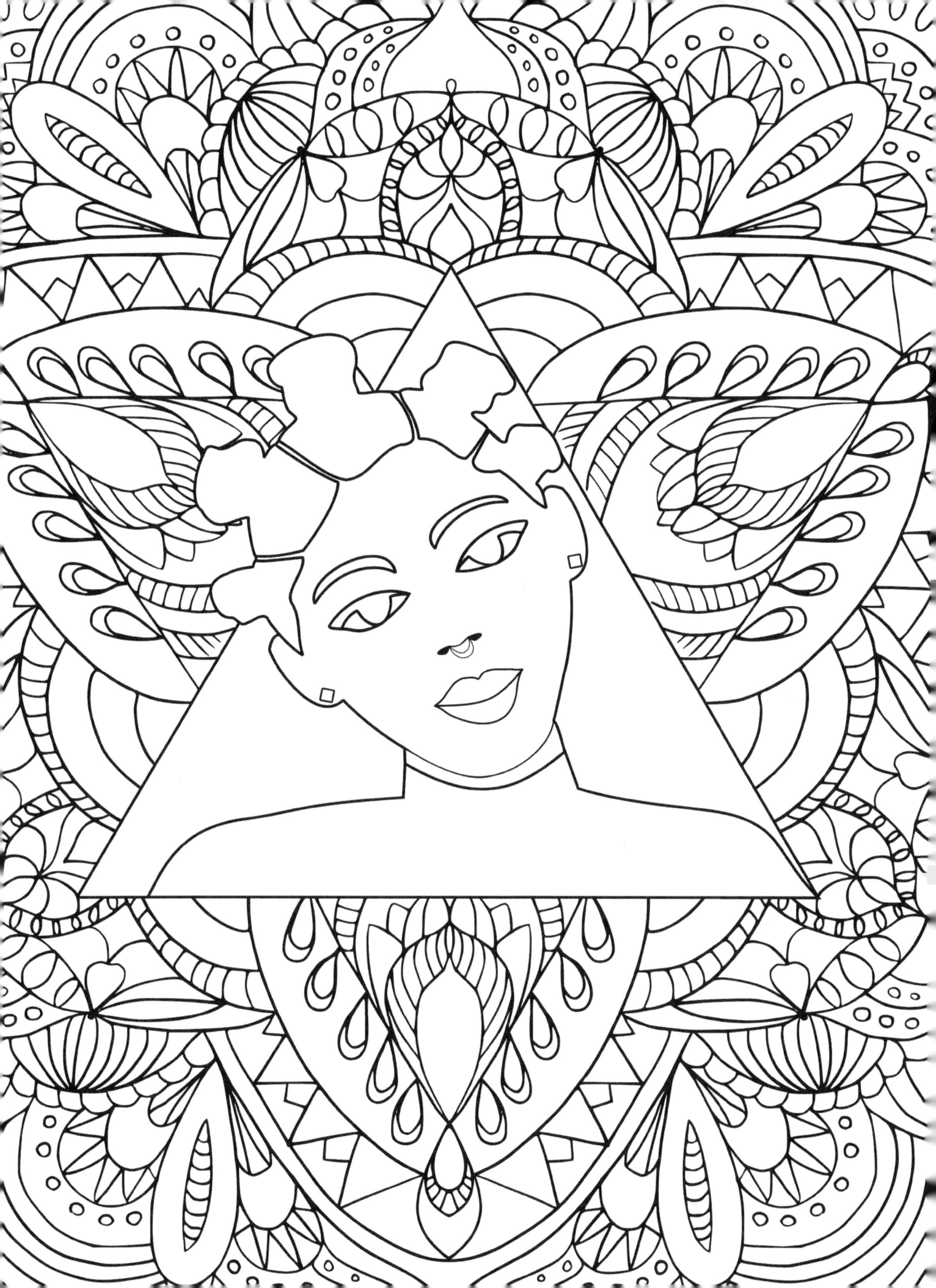

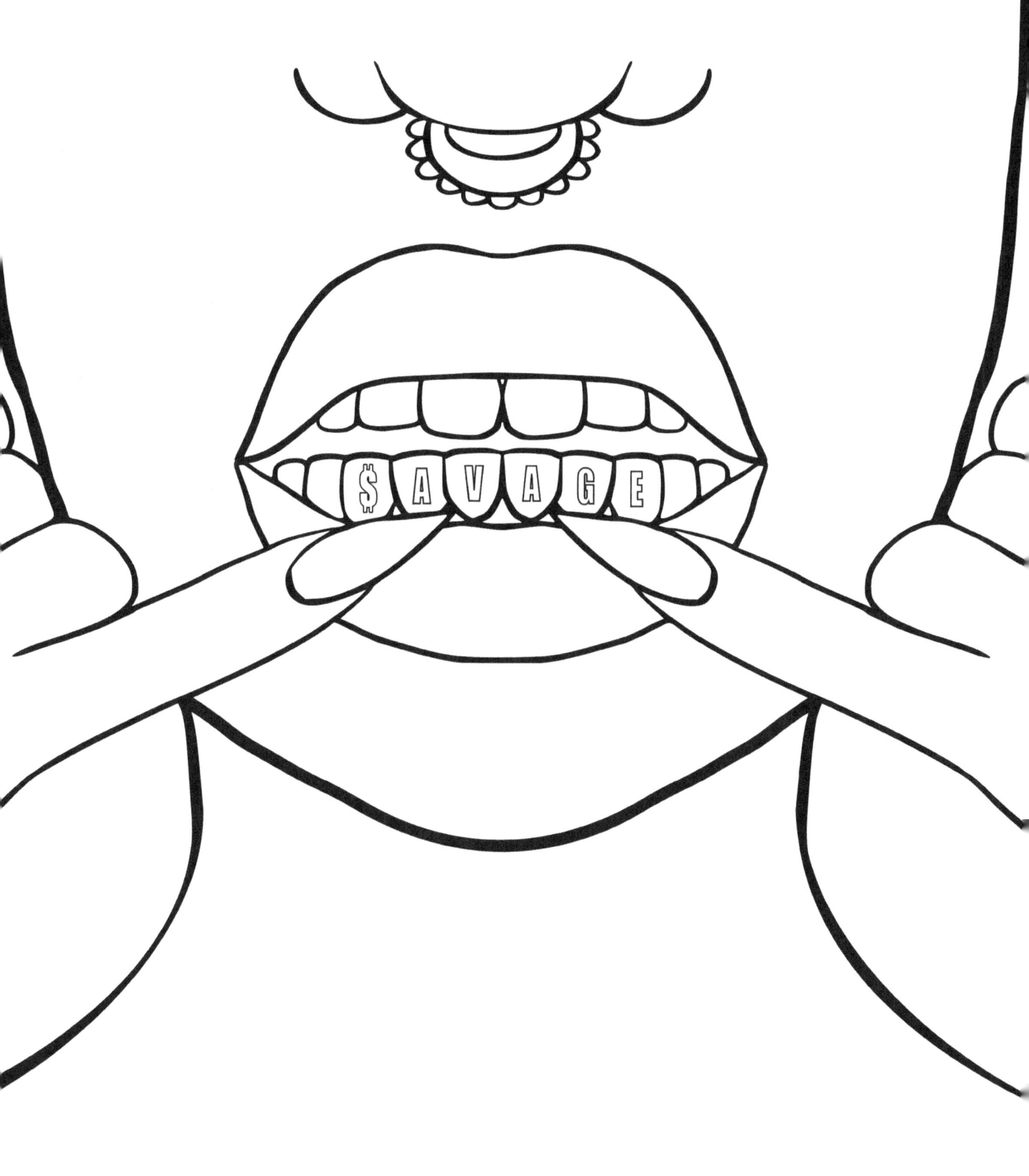

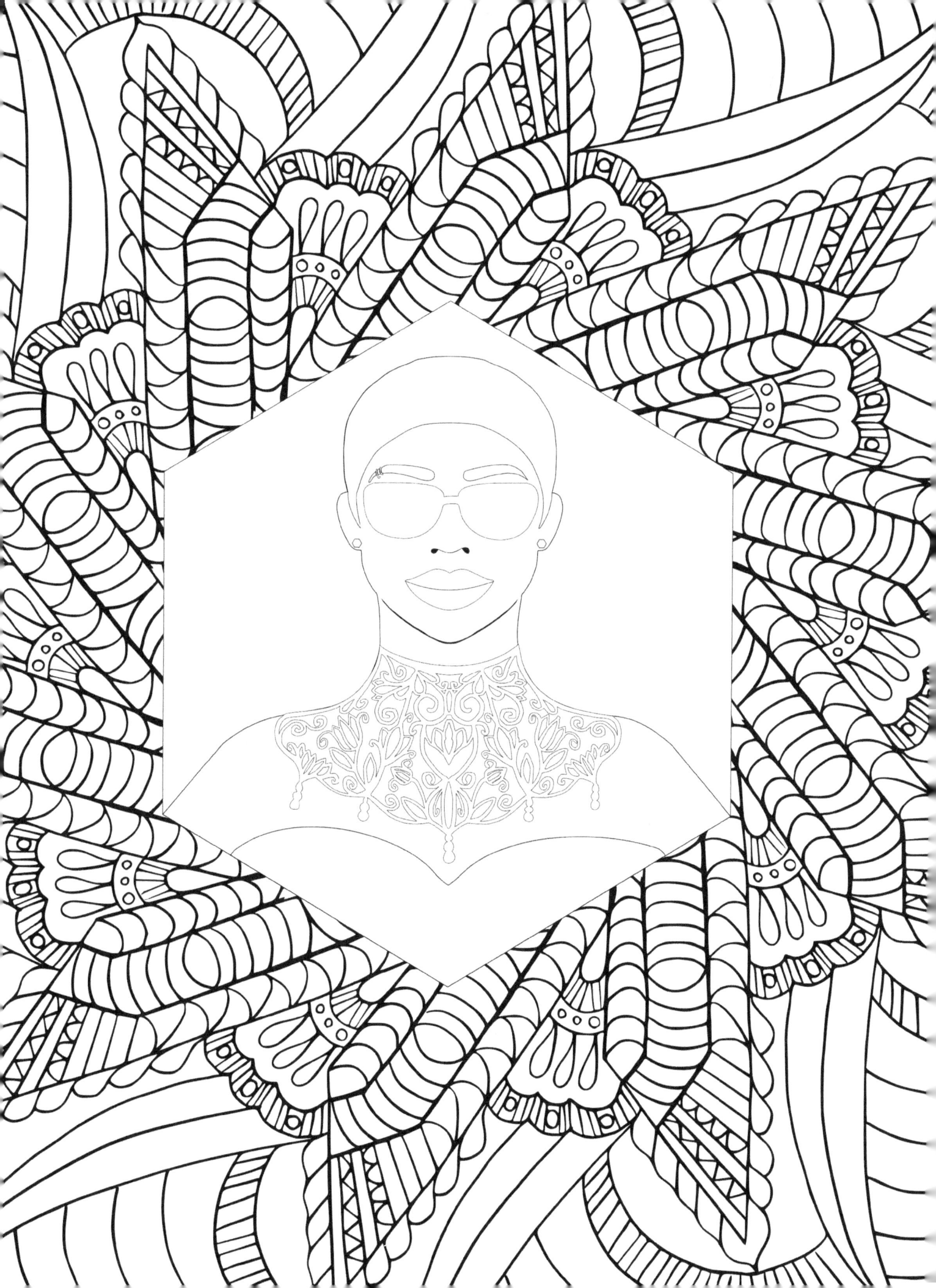

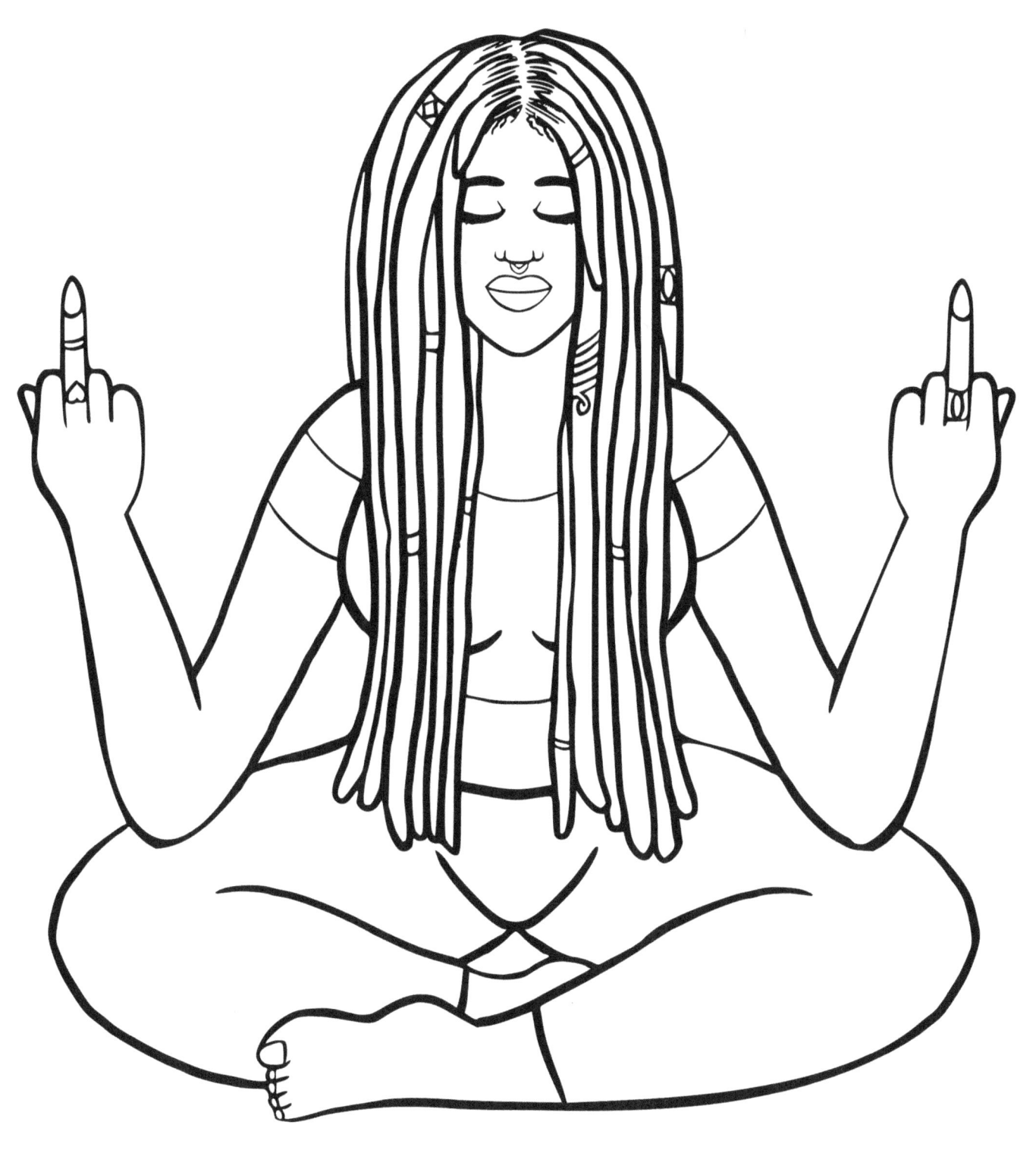

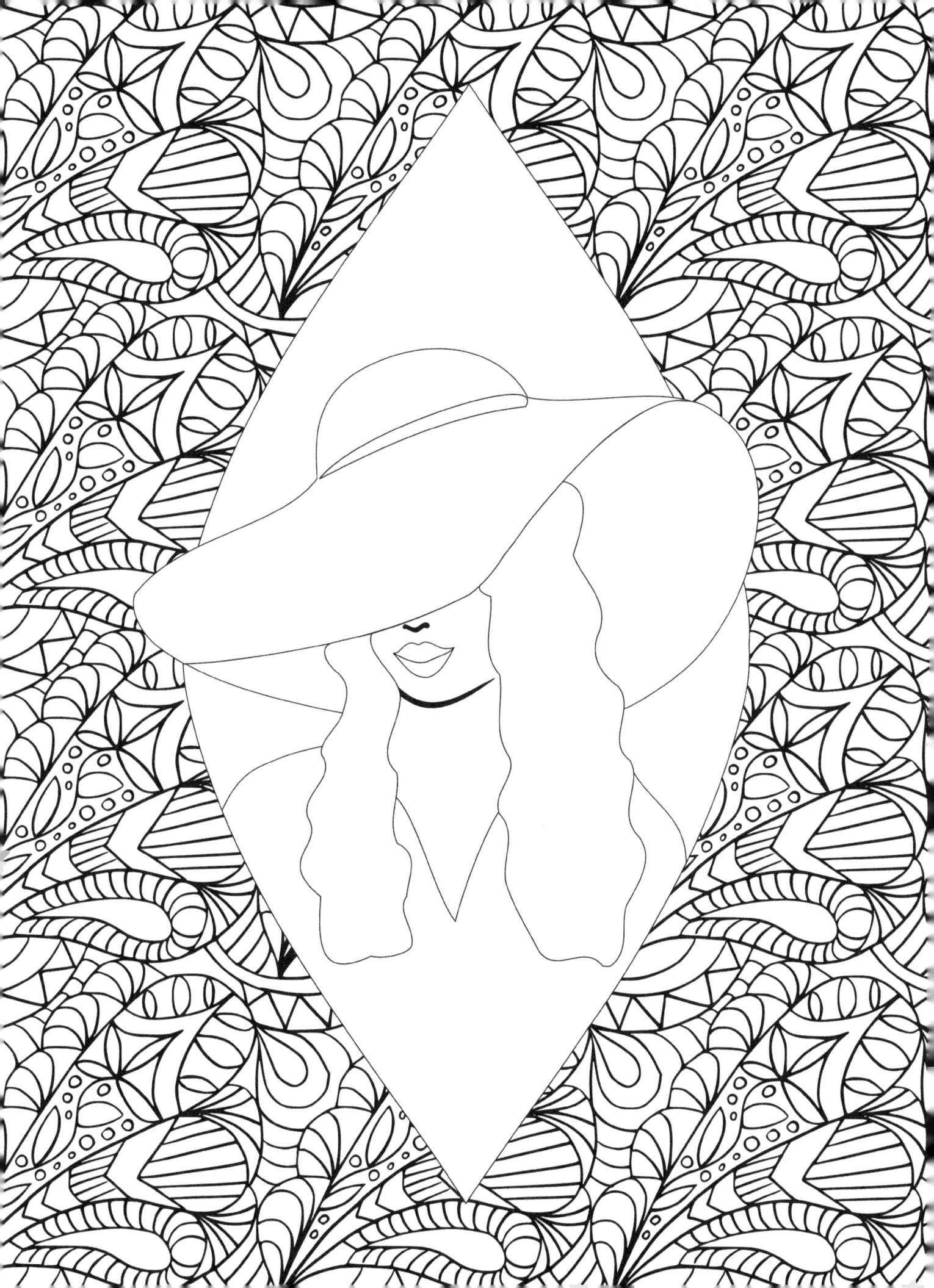

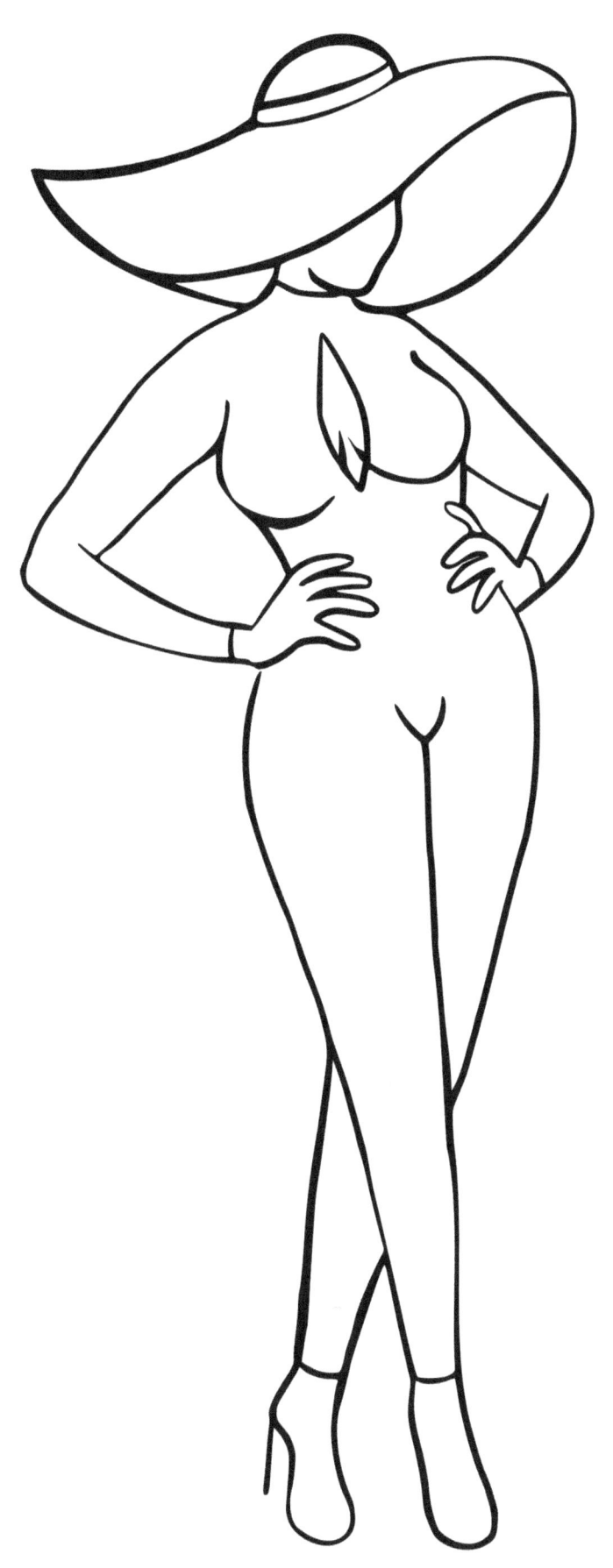

sundays are for servin

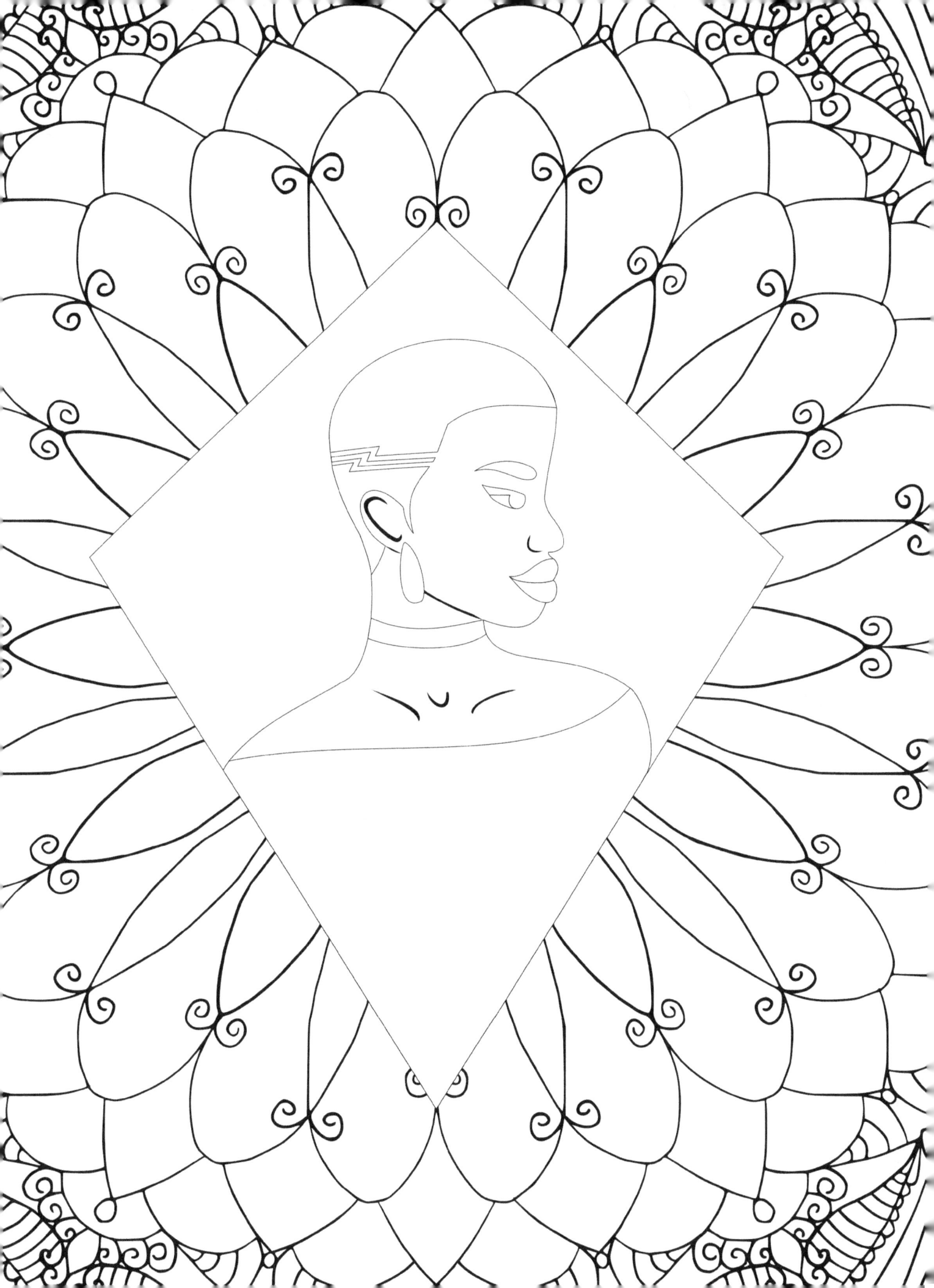

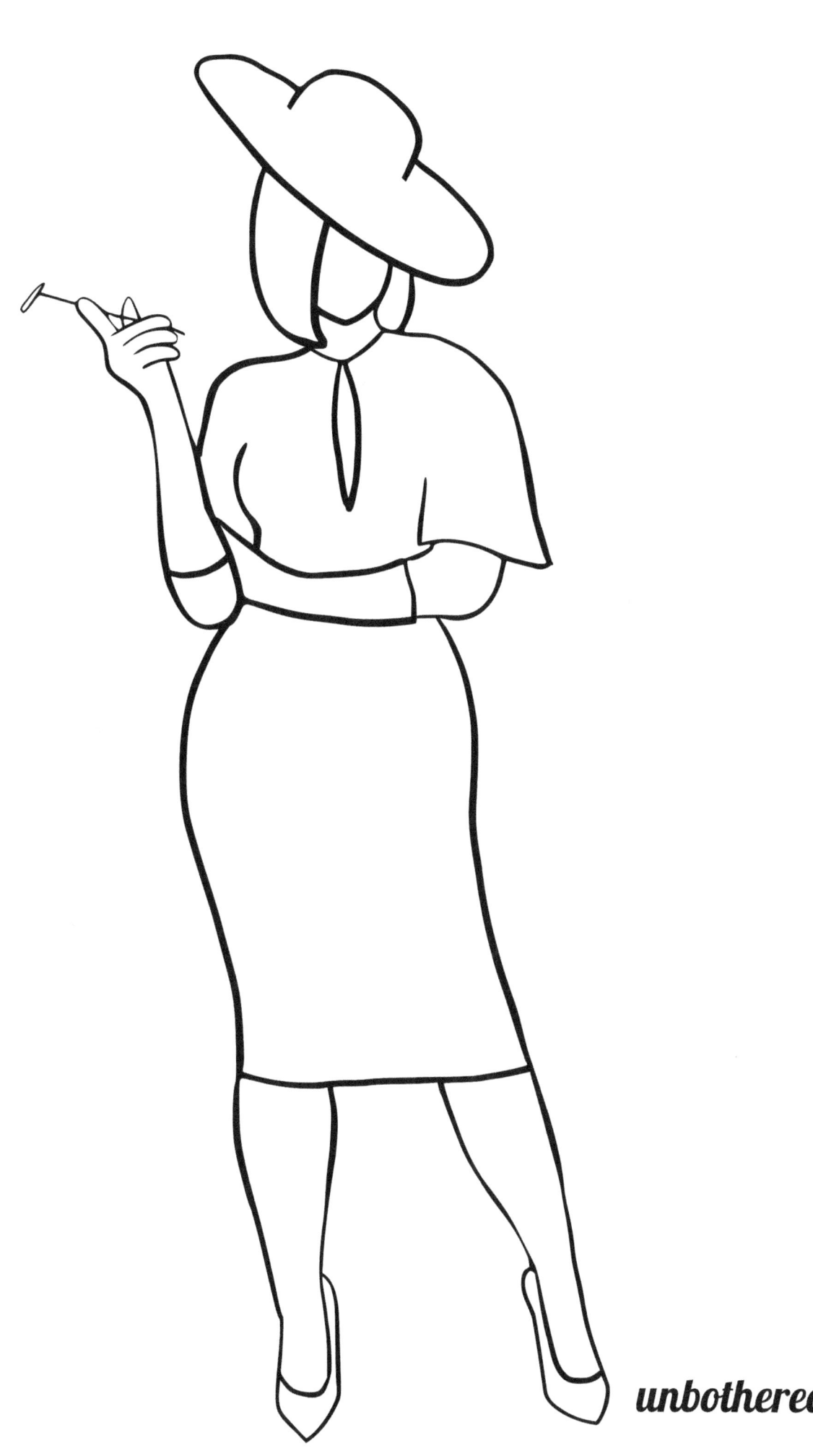

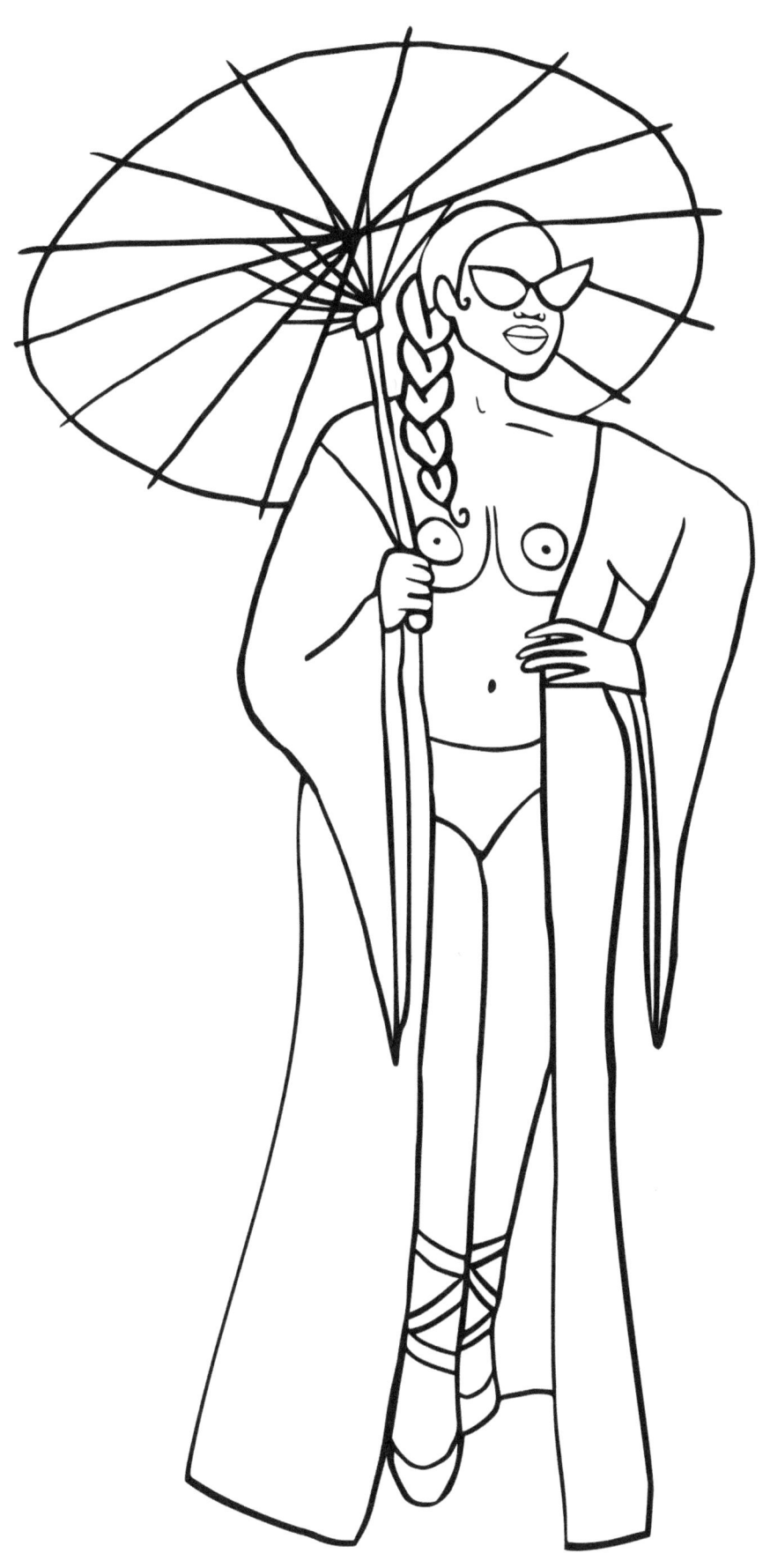

Big areola mood

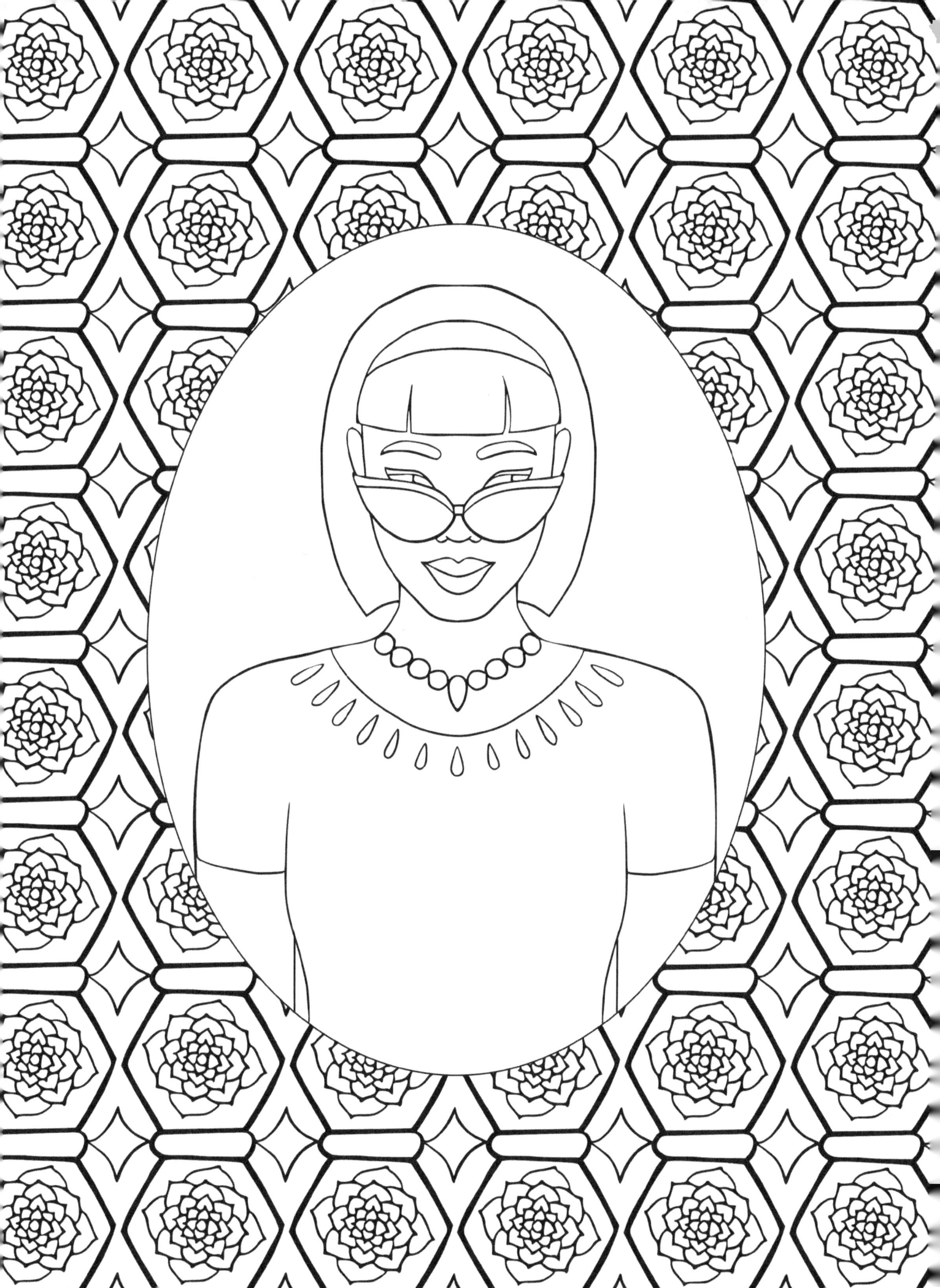

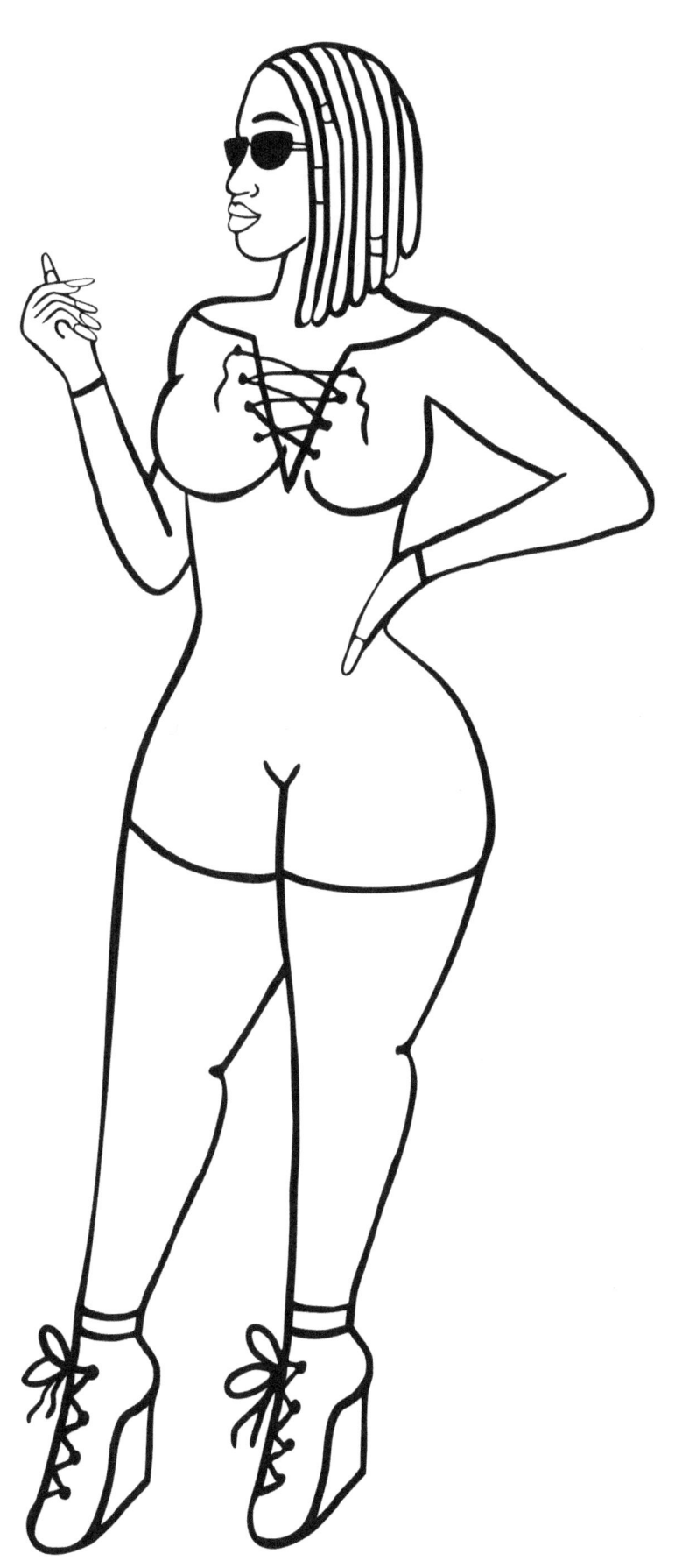

a lil bougie a lil hood

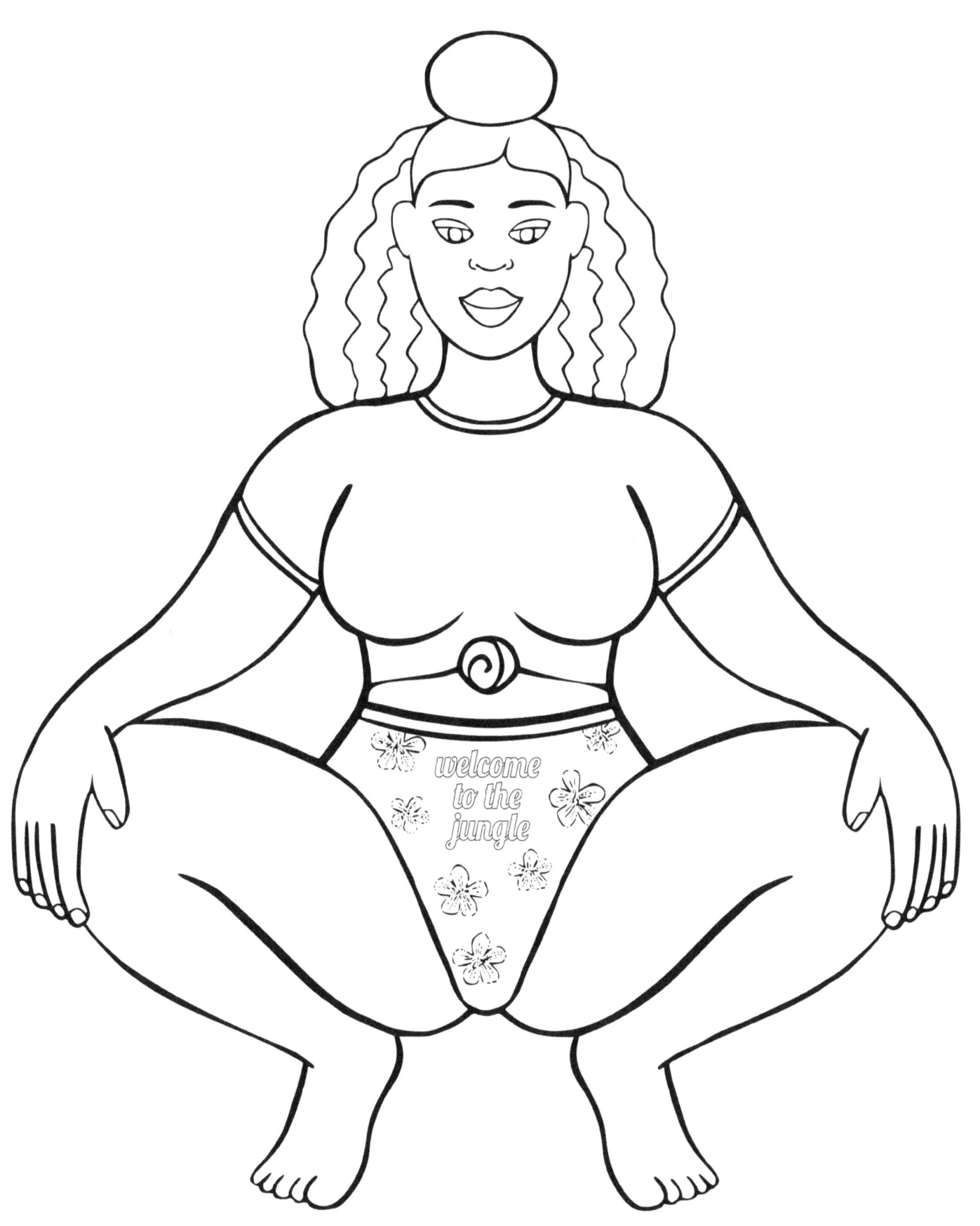

welcome to the jungle: wet, wild n warm

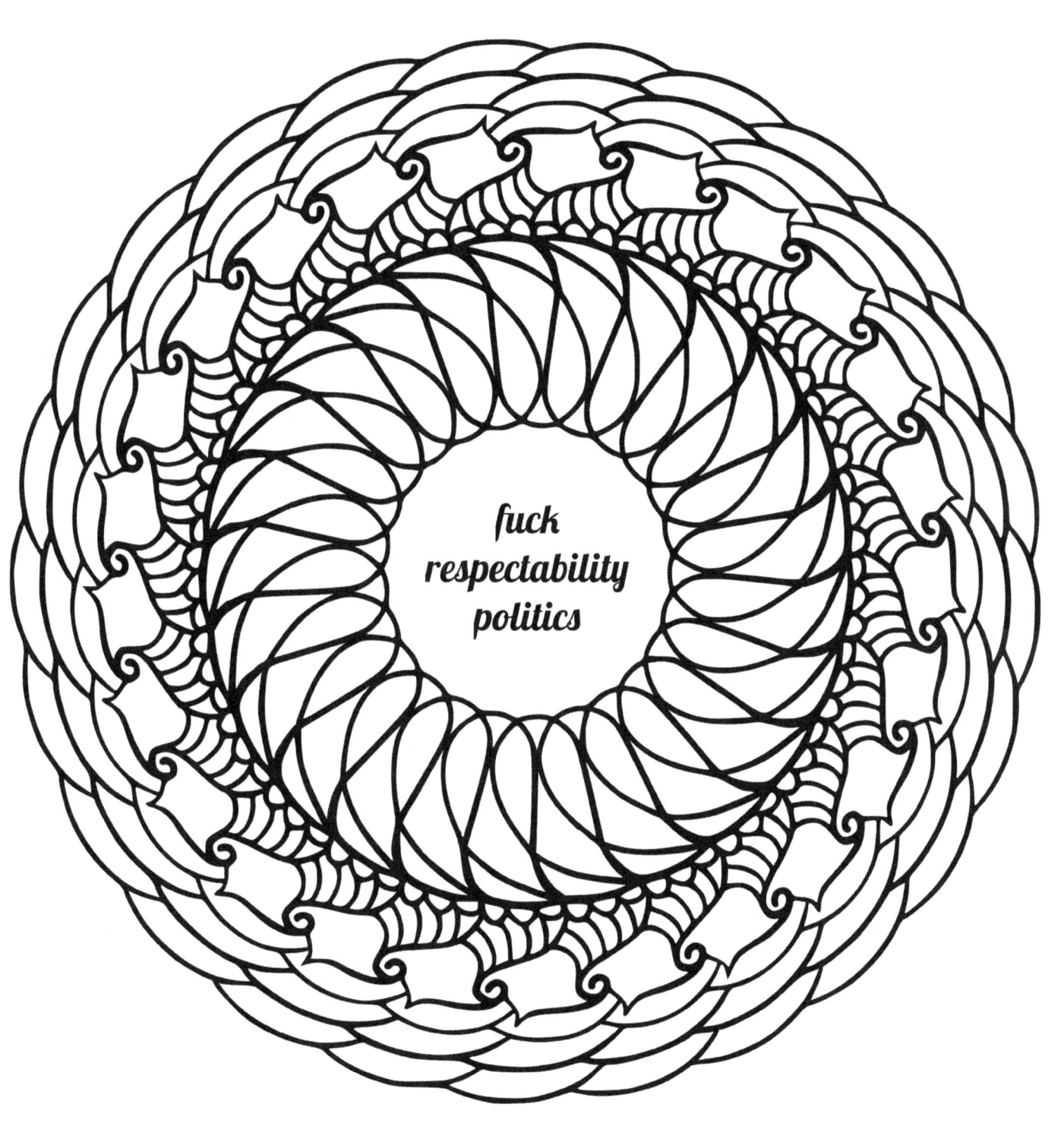

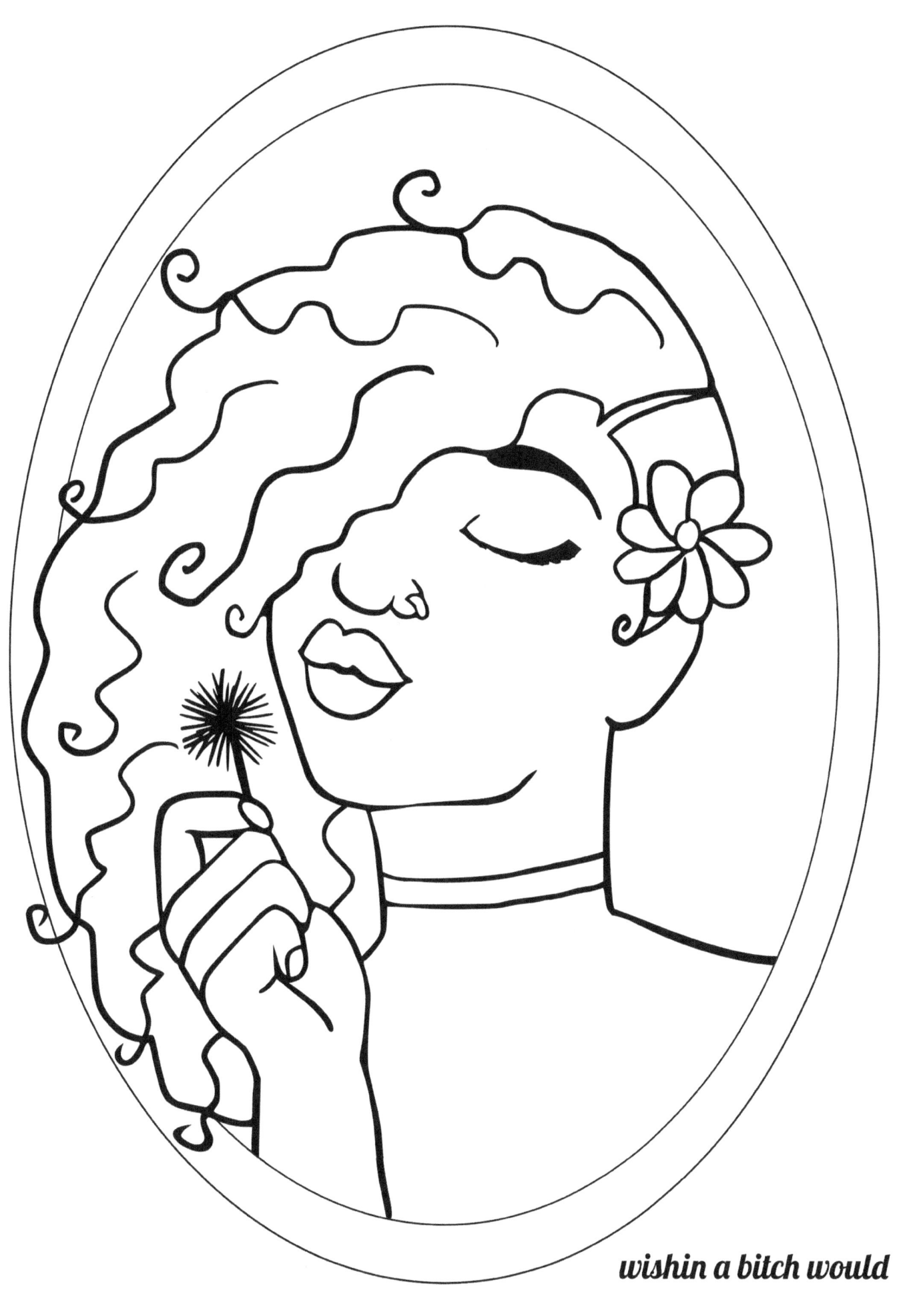

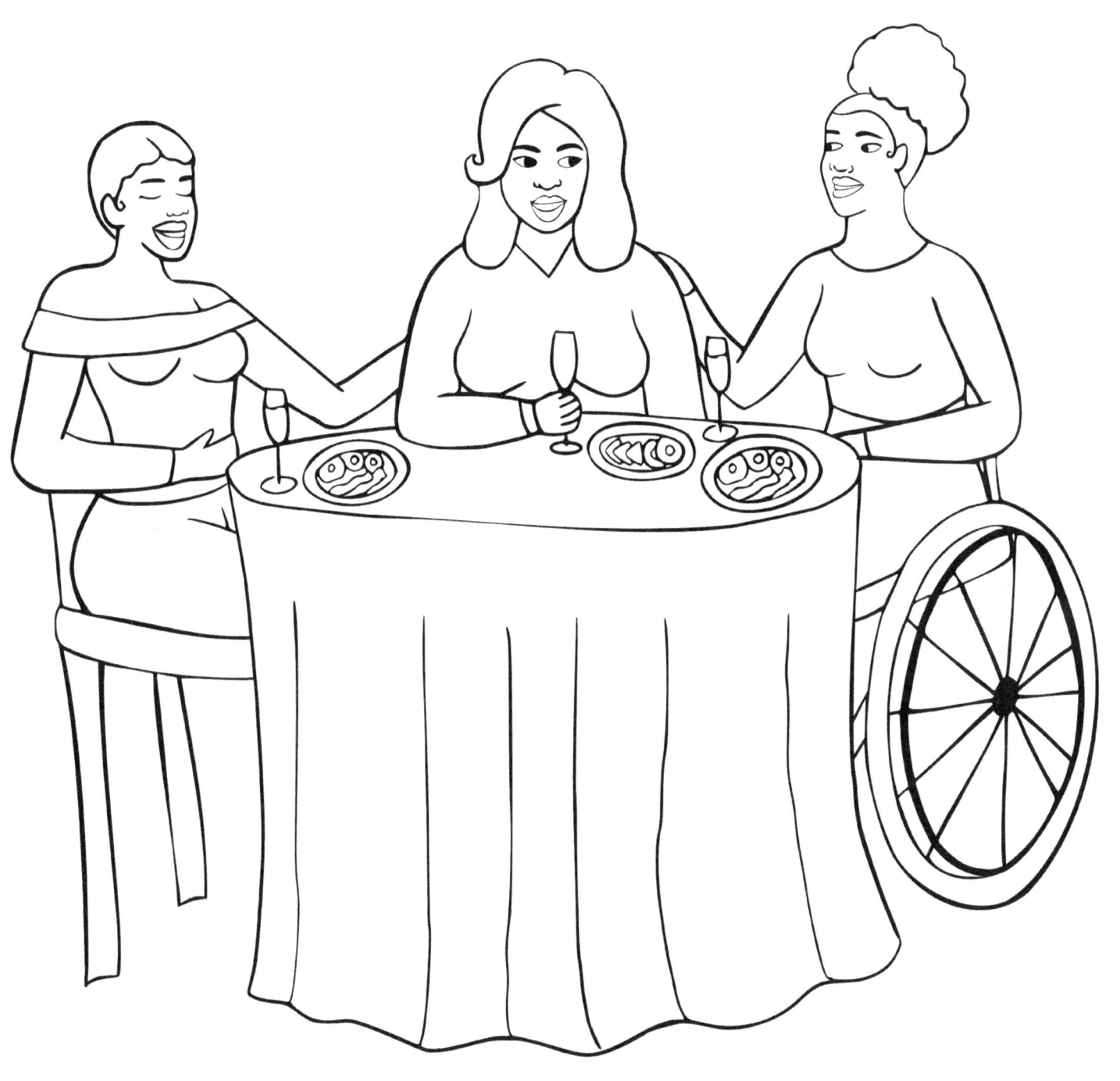

dishin about last night

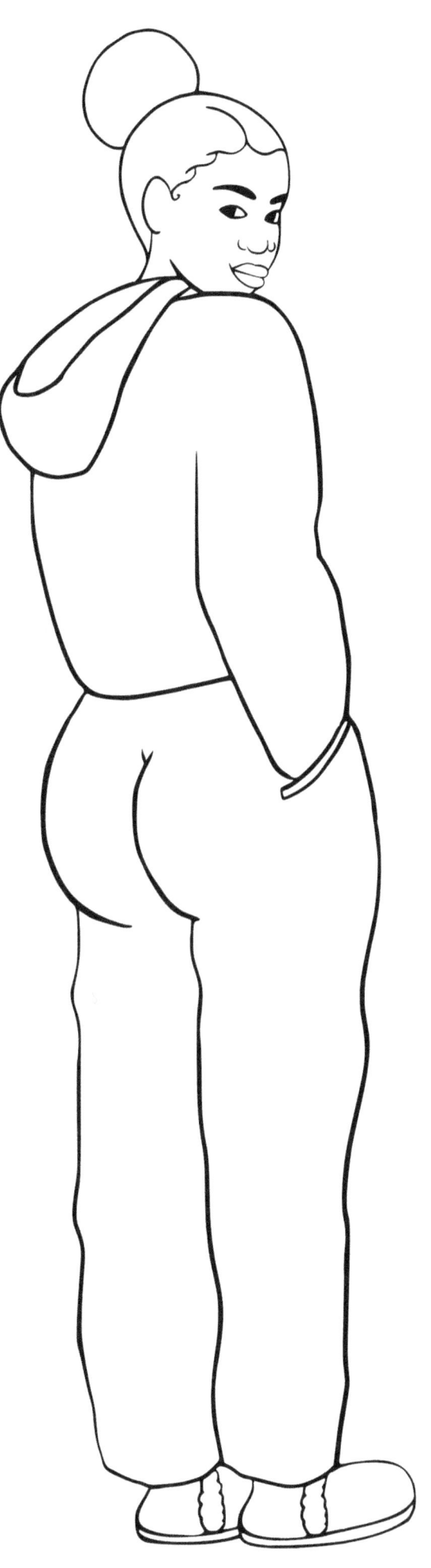

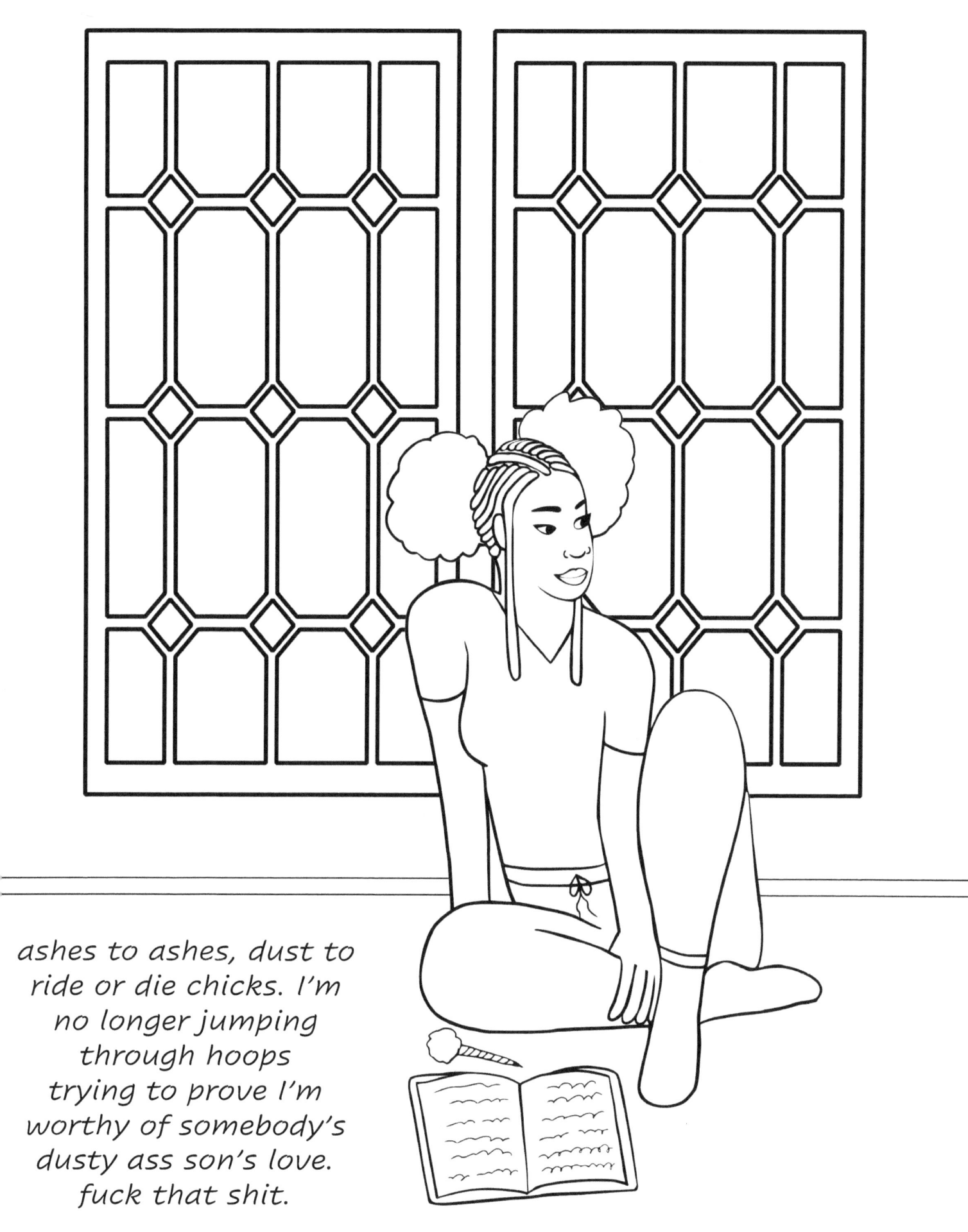

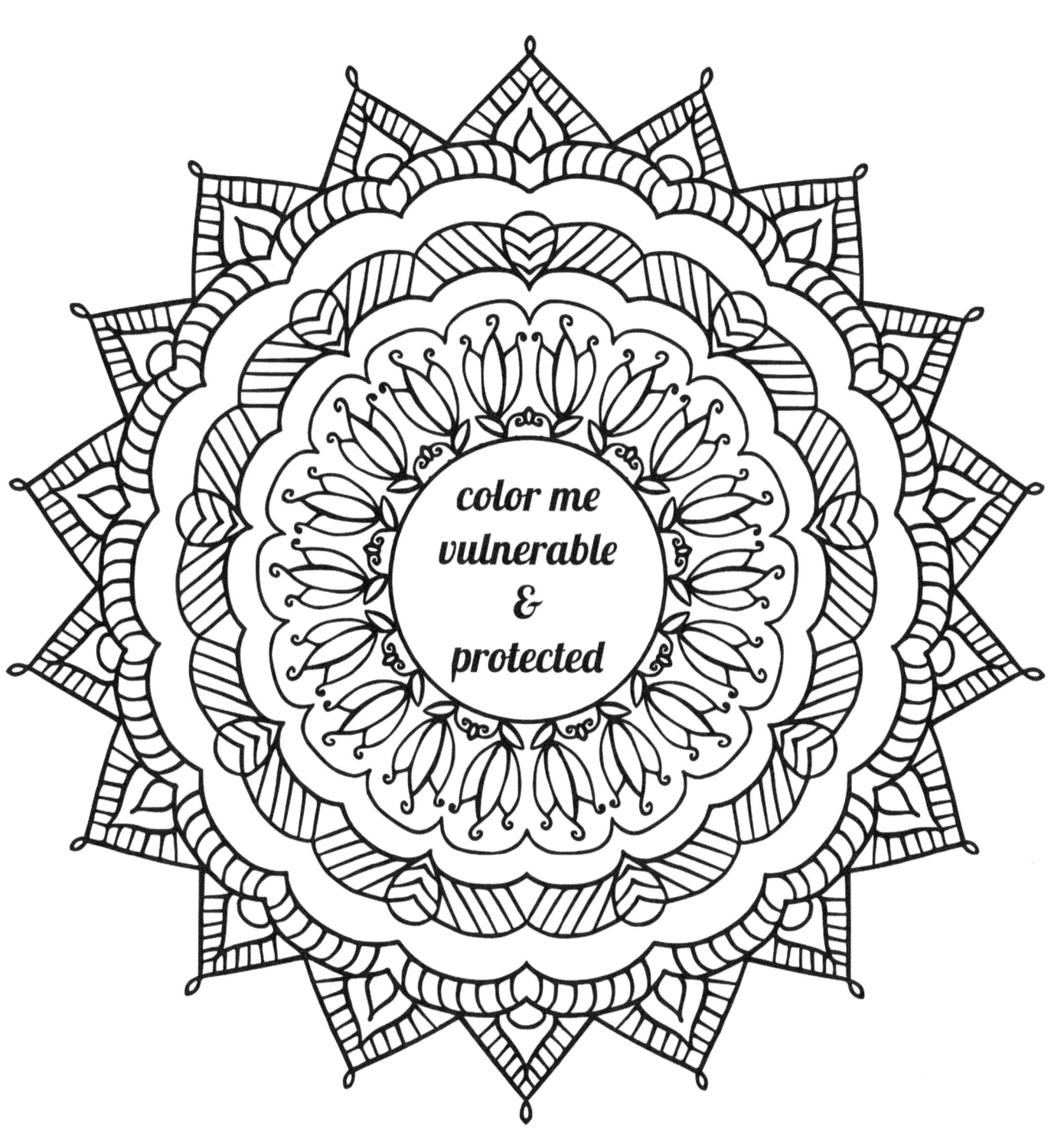

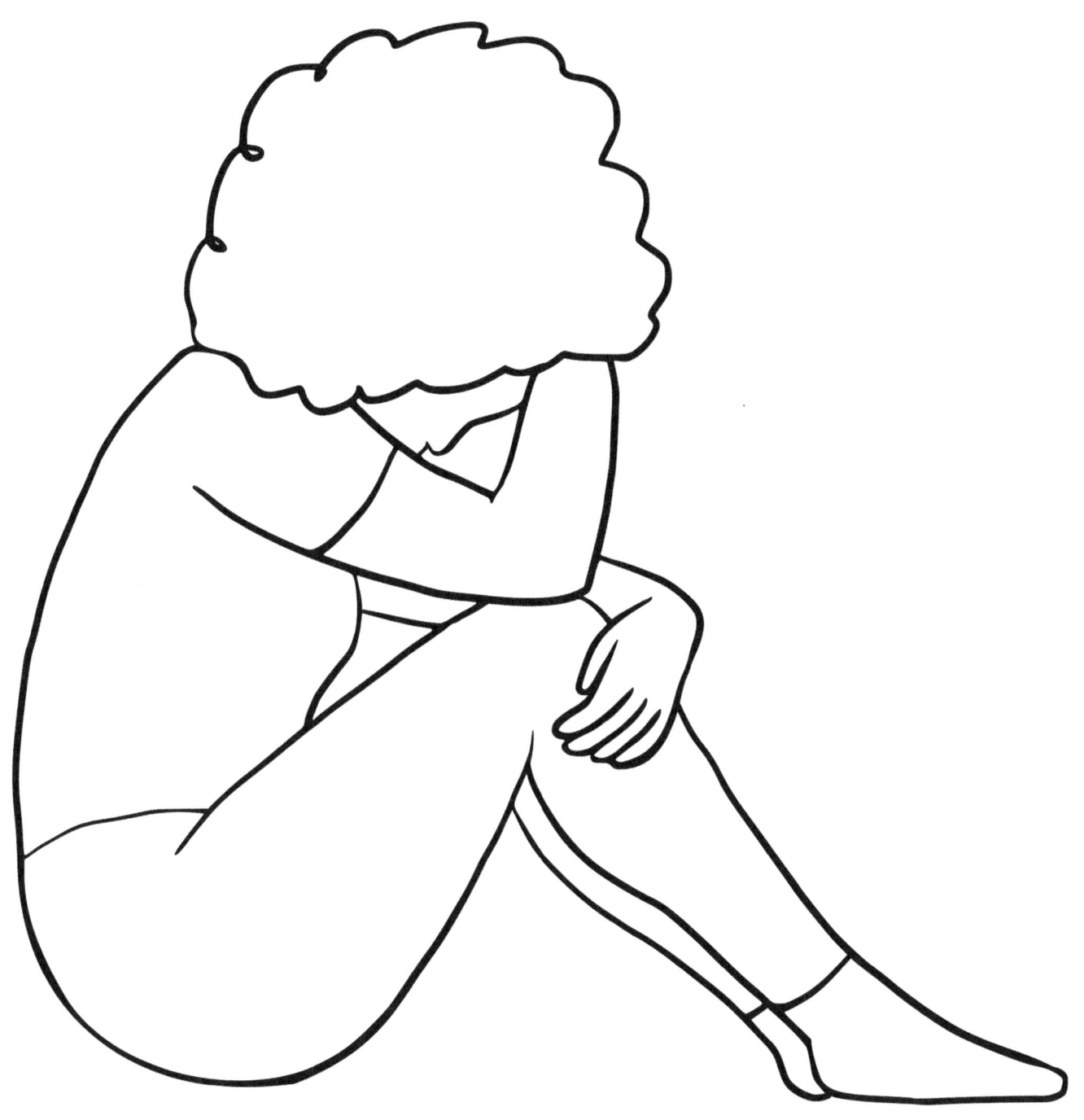

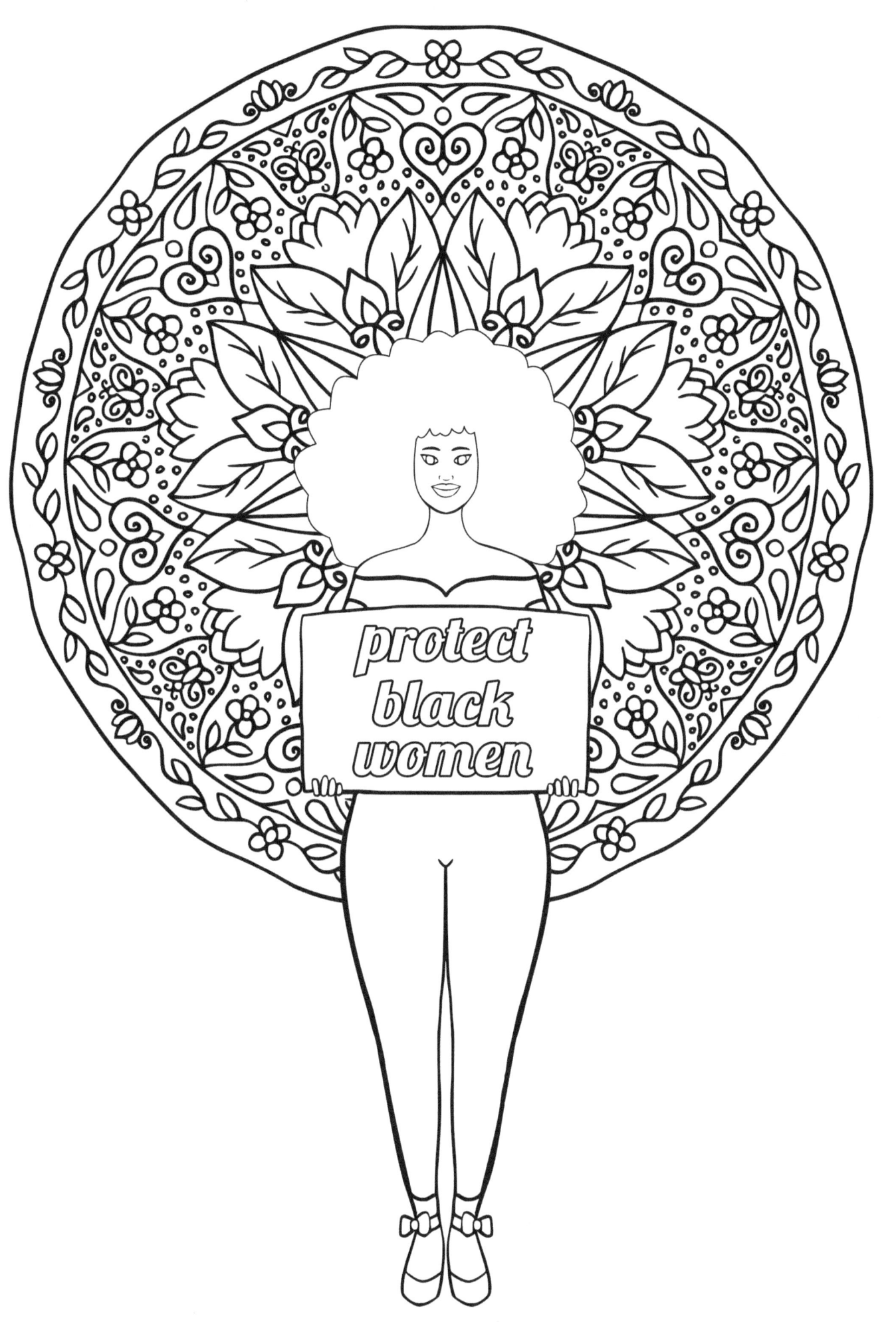

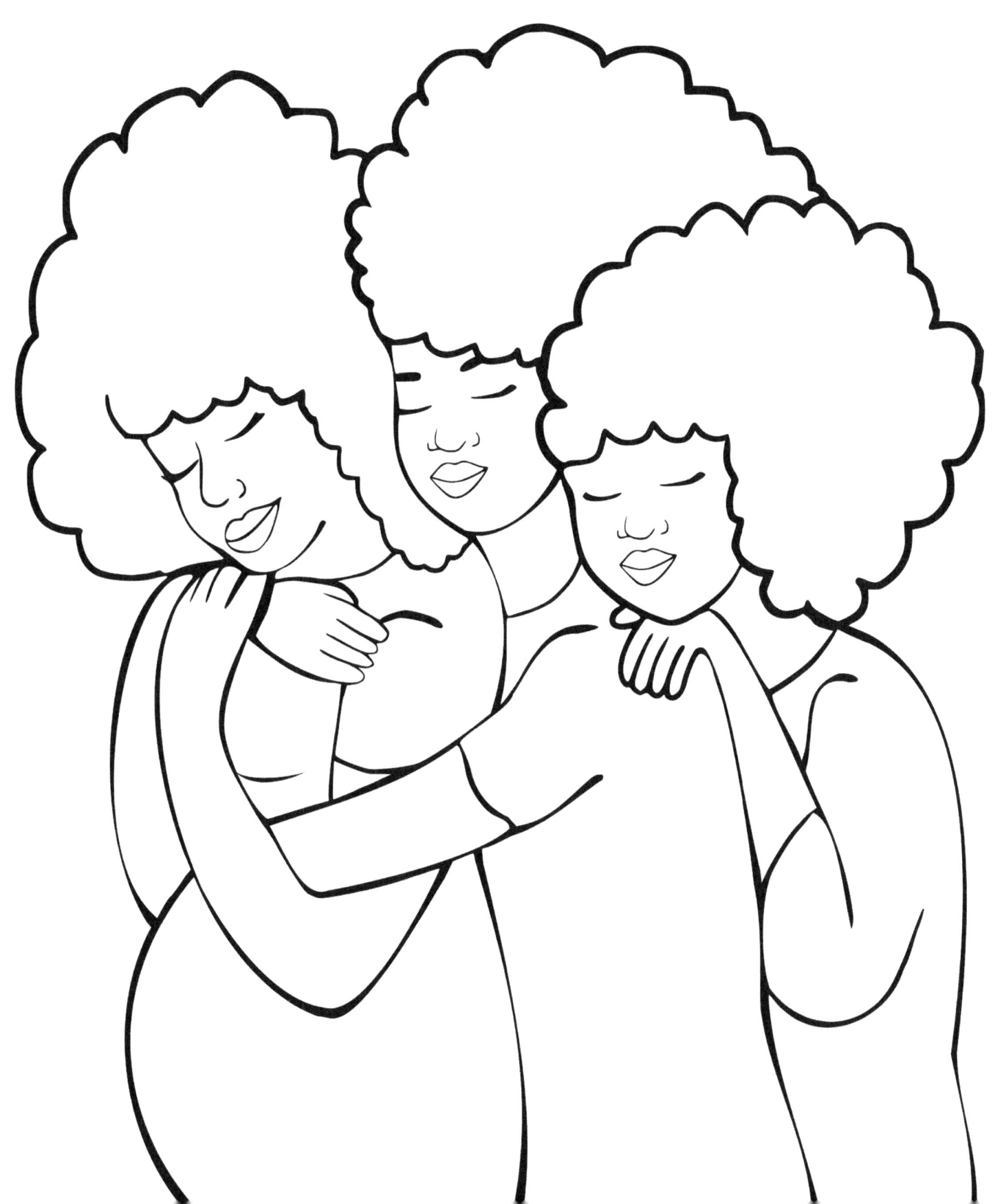

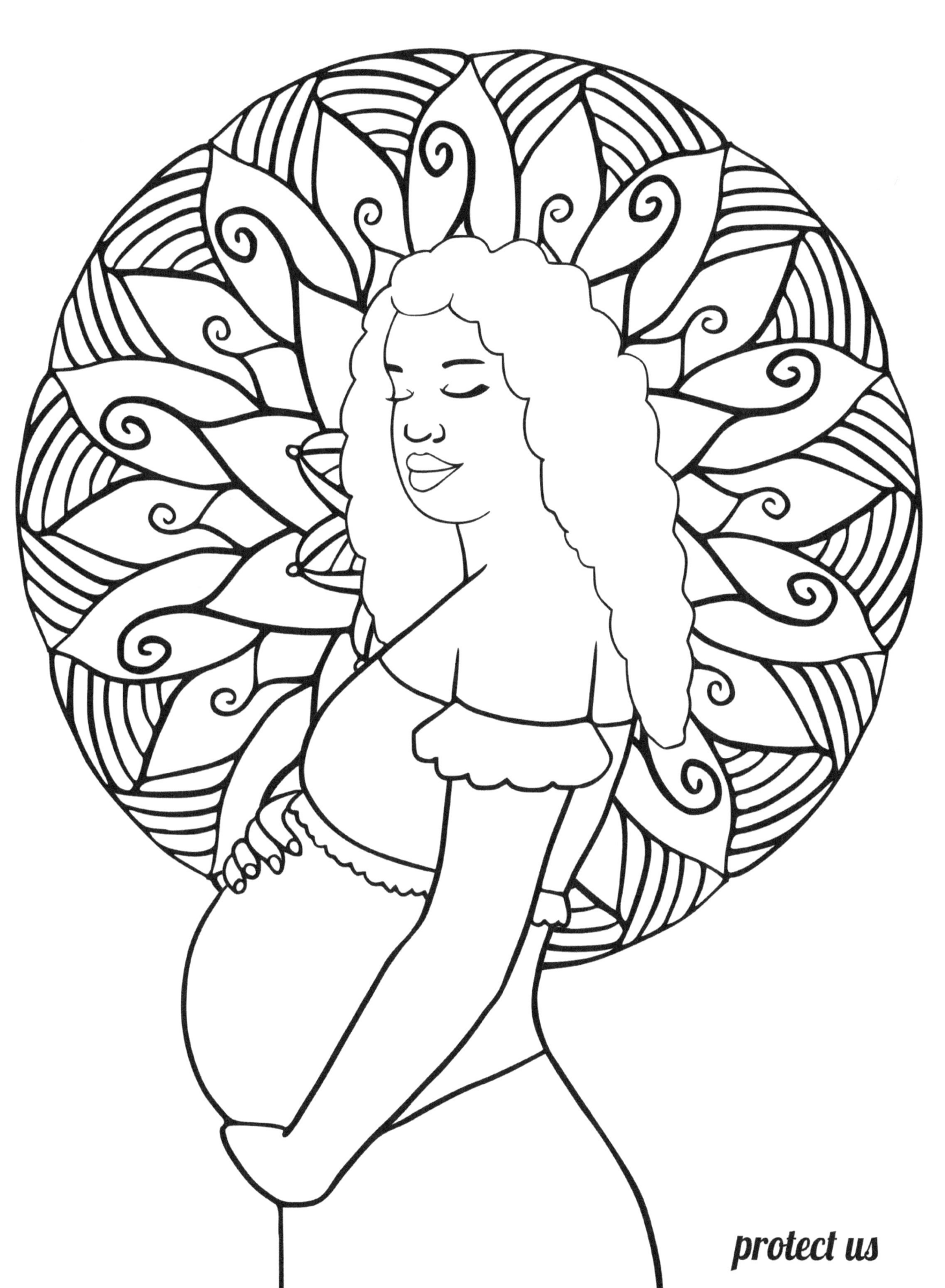

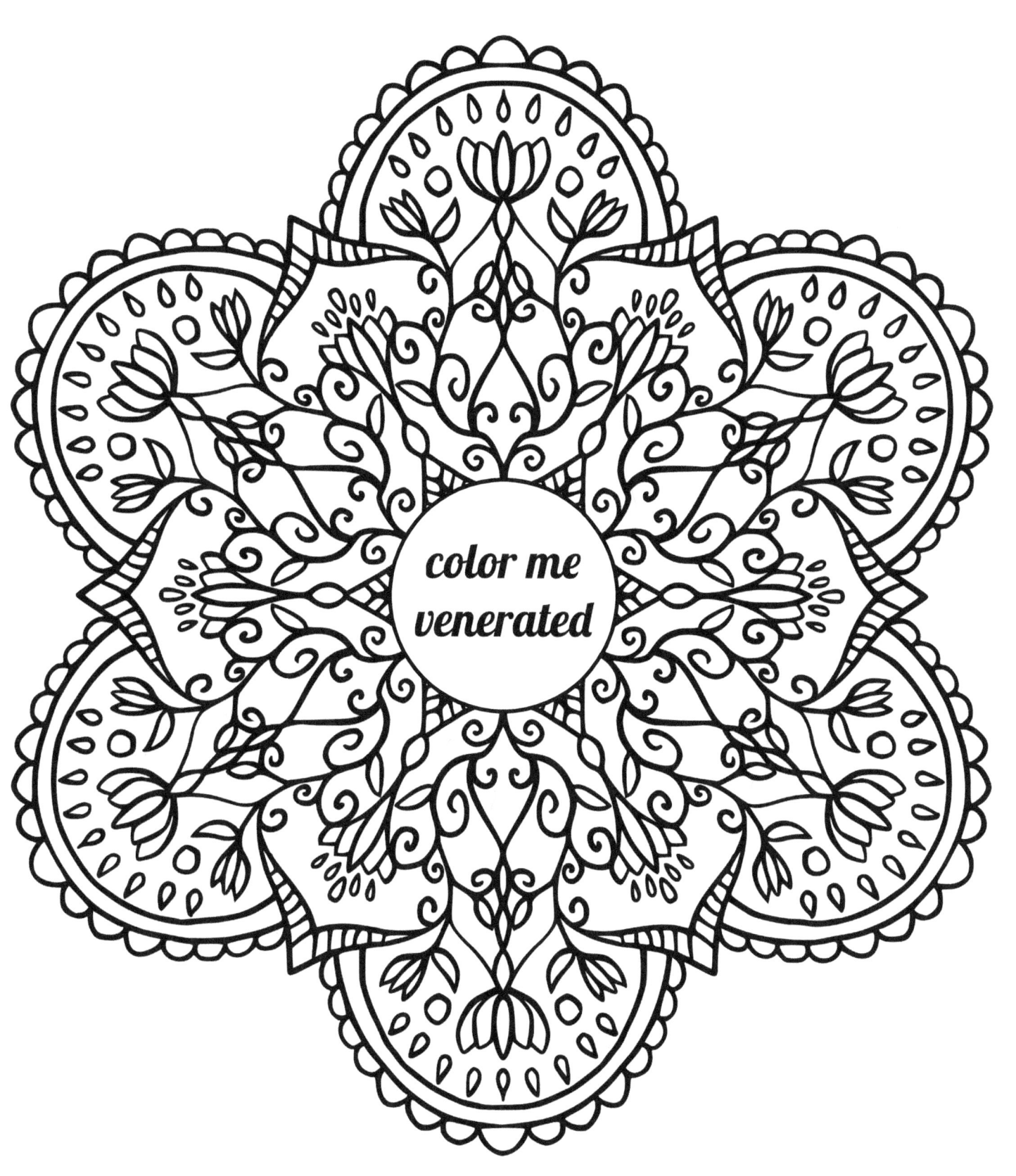

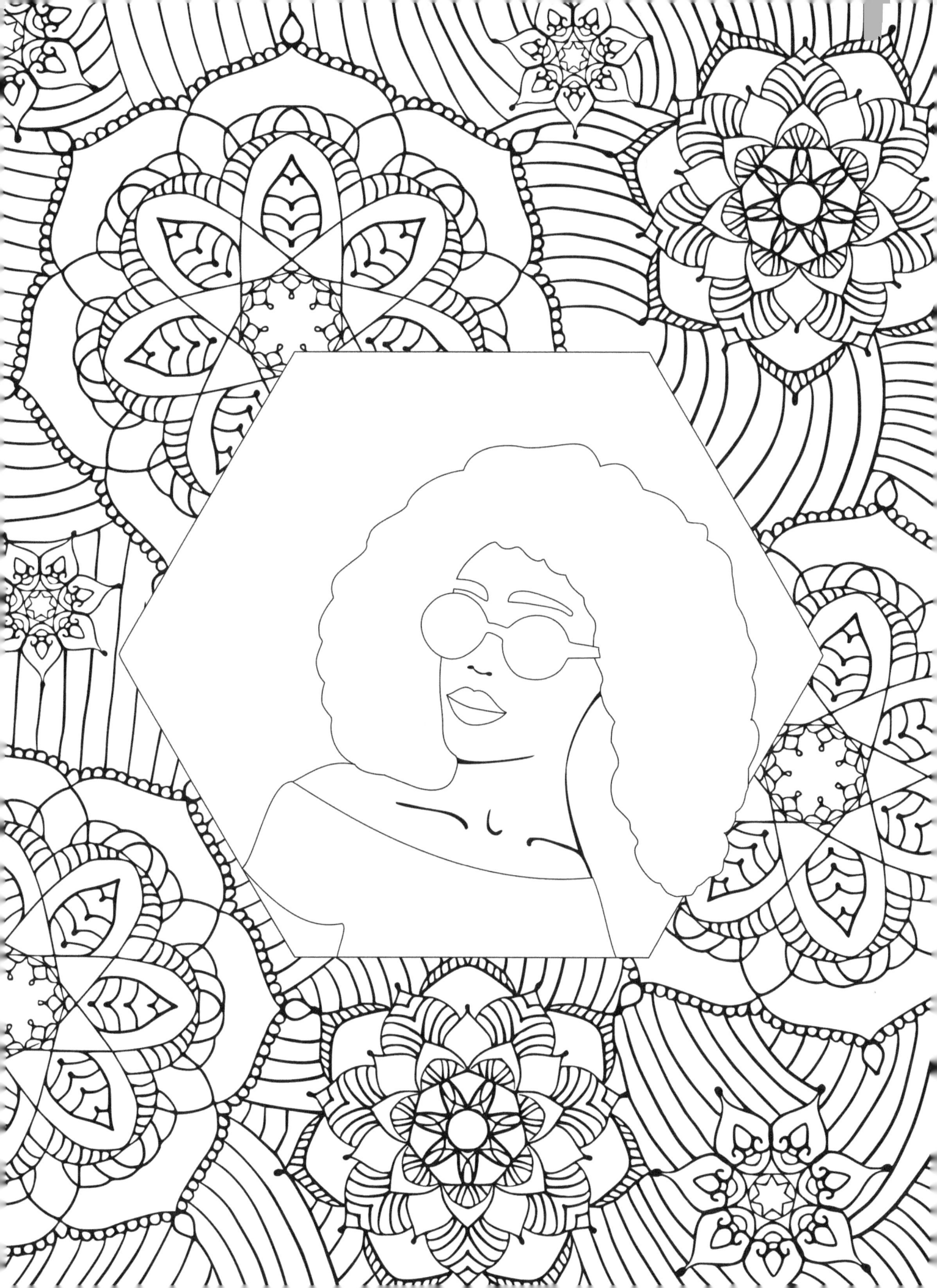

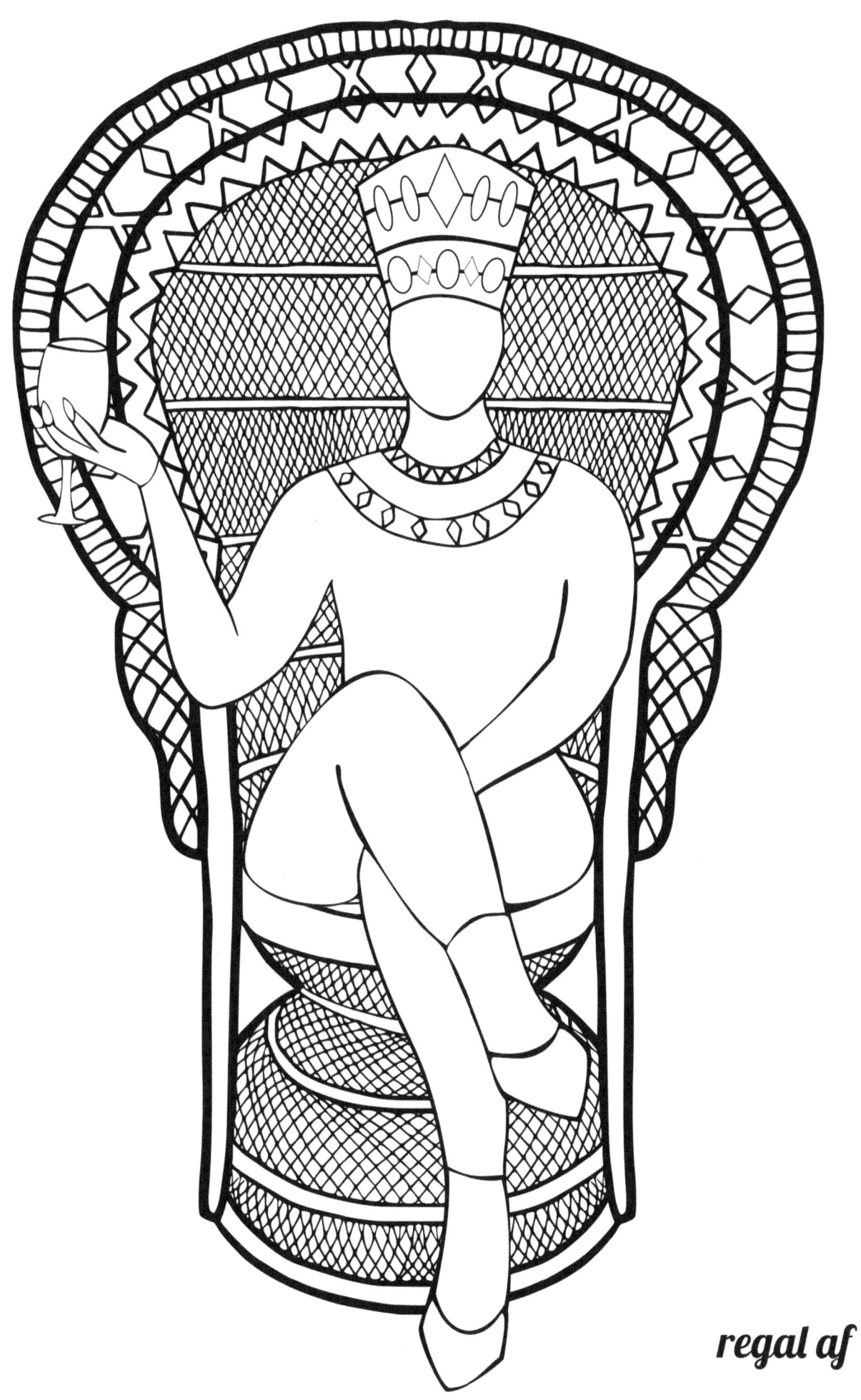

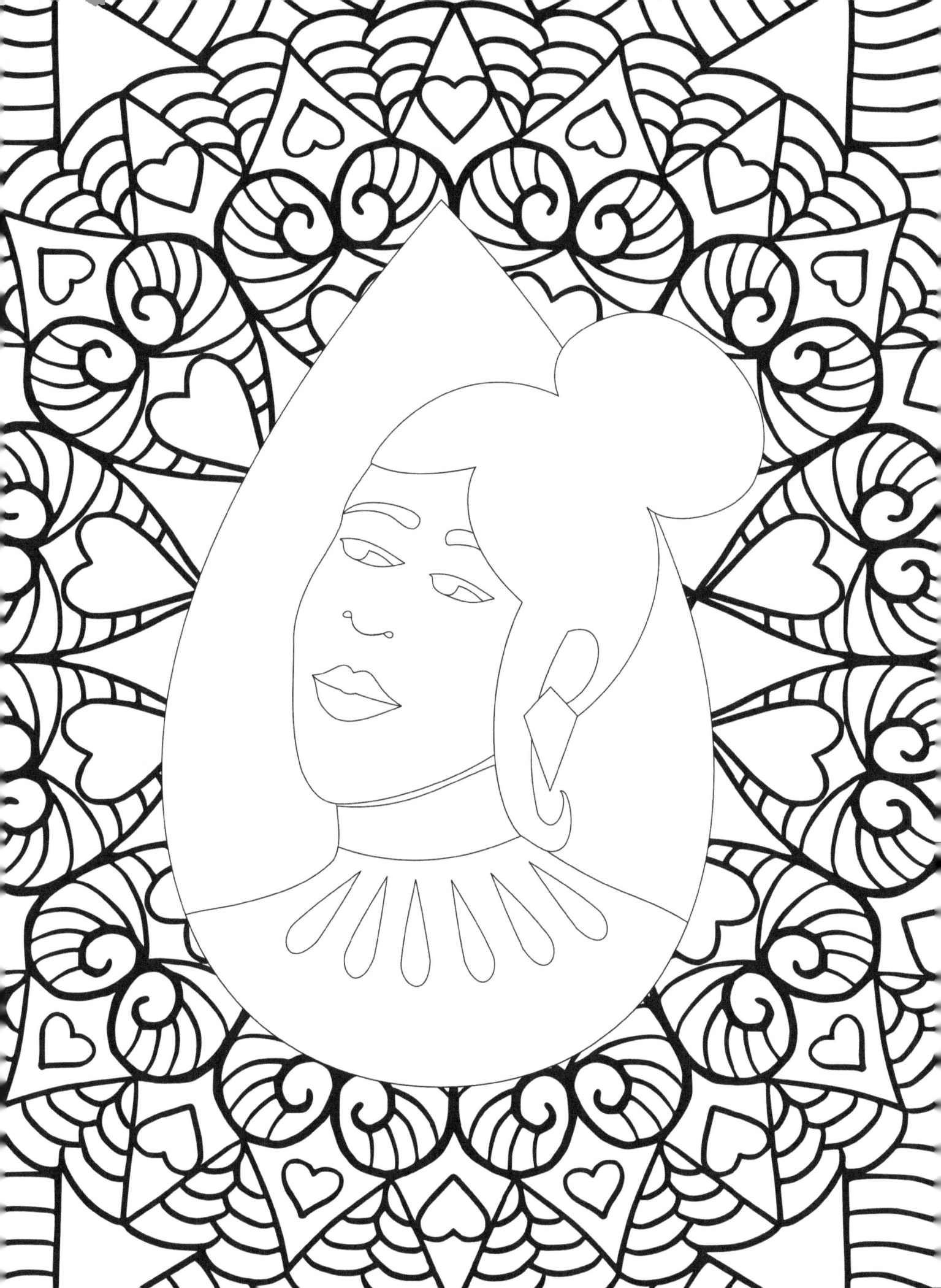

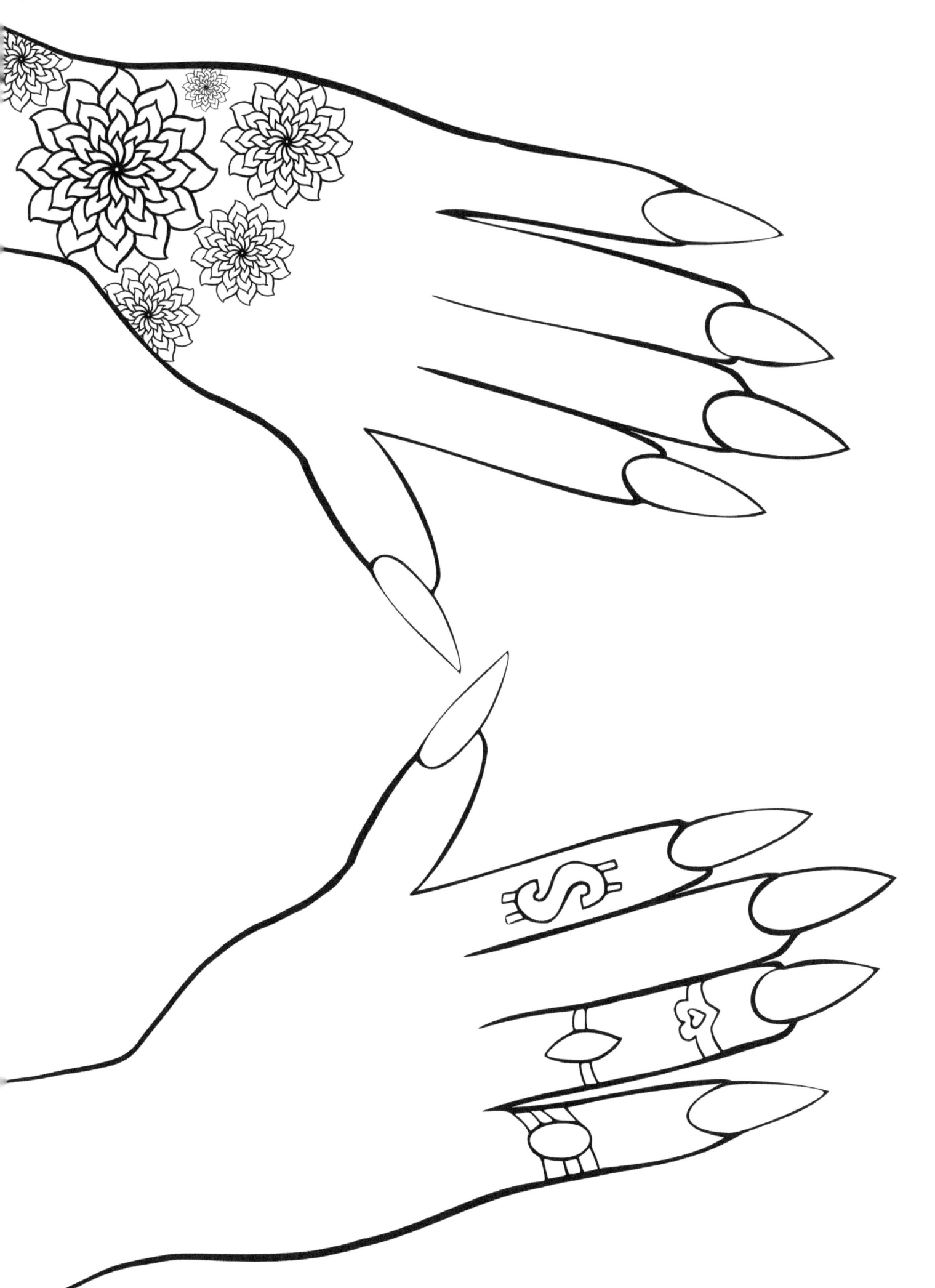

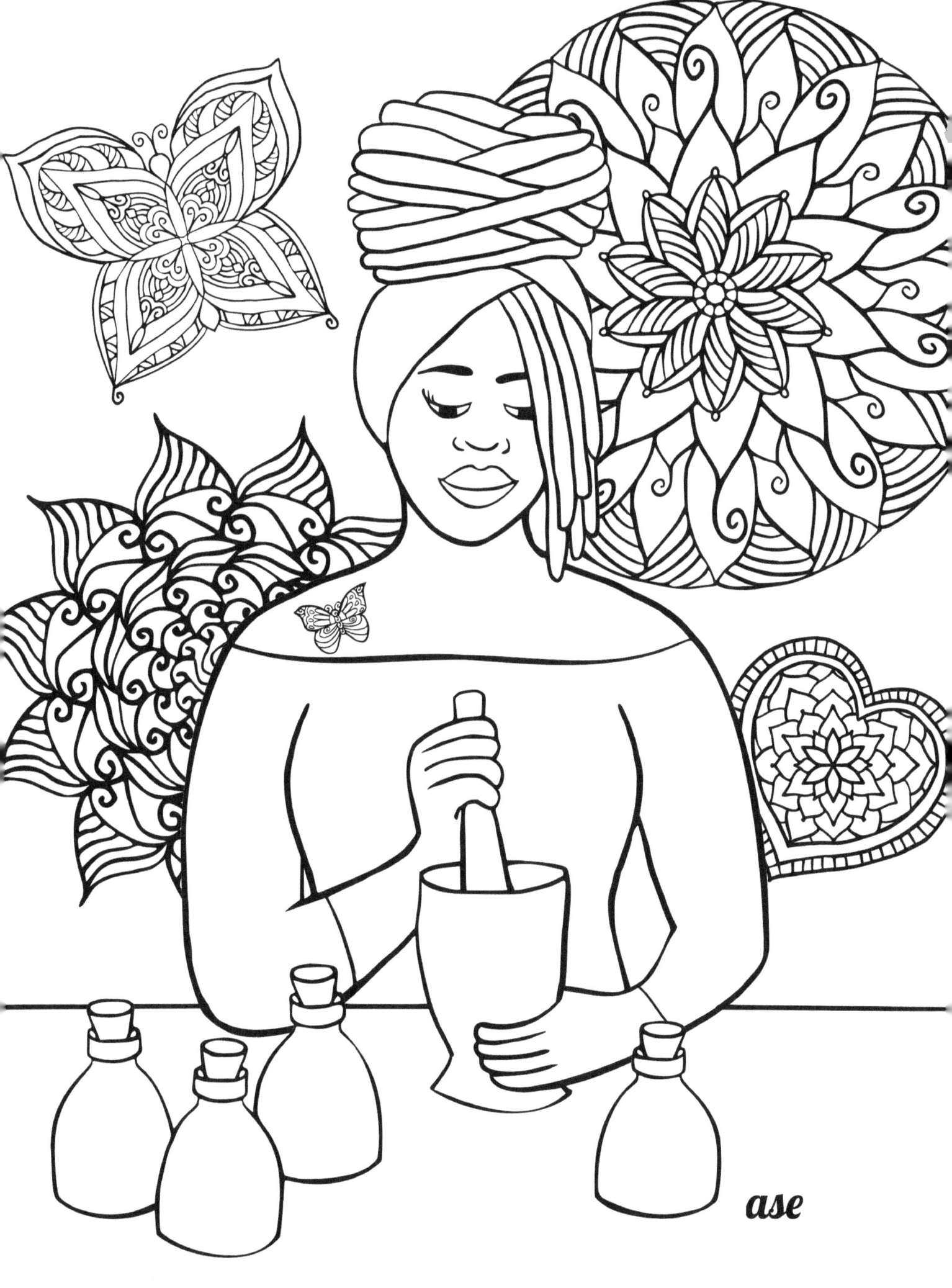

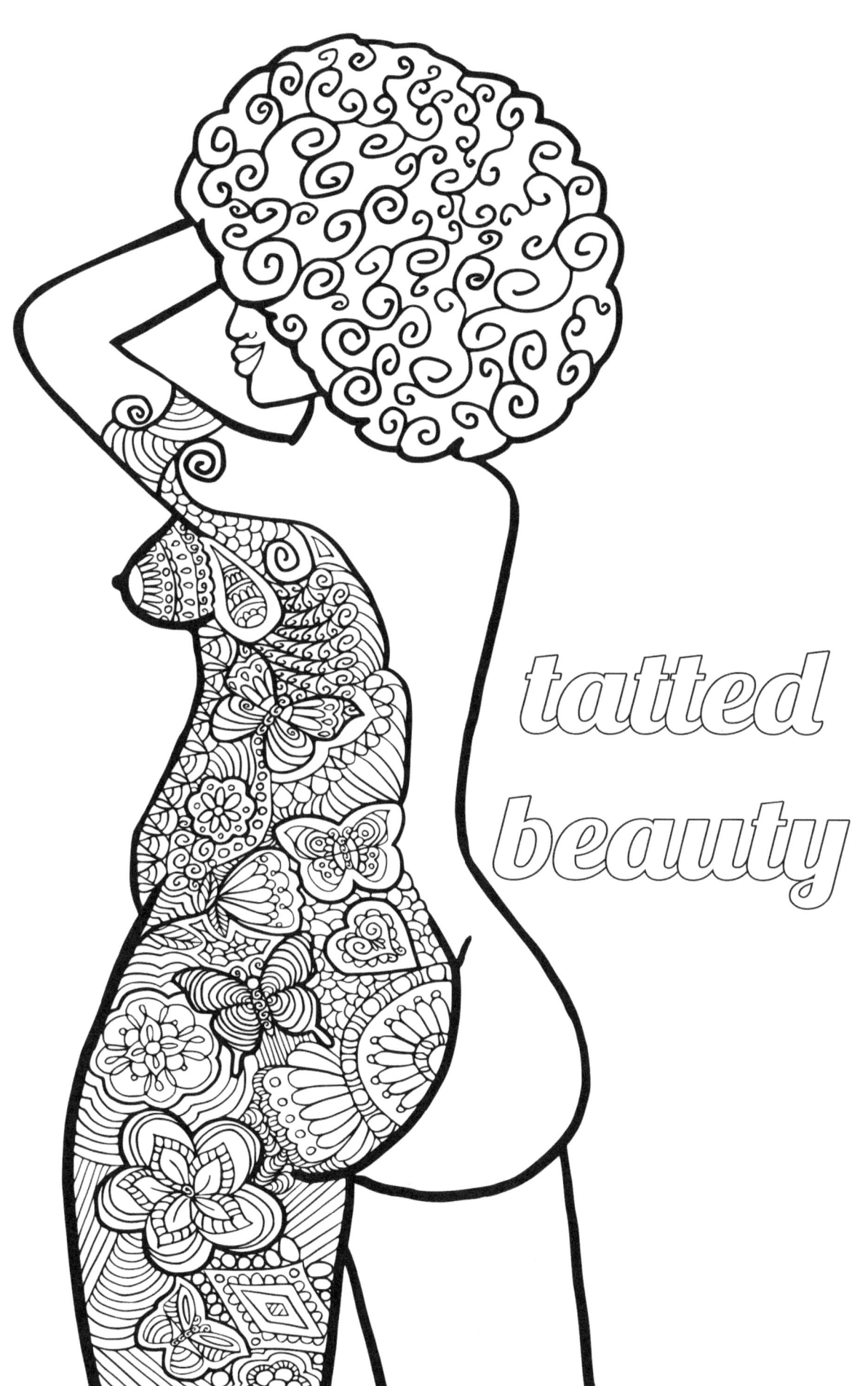

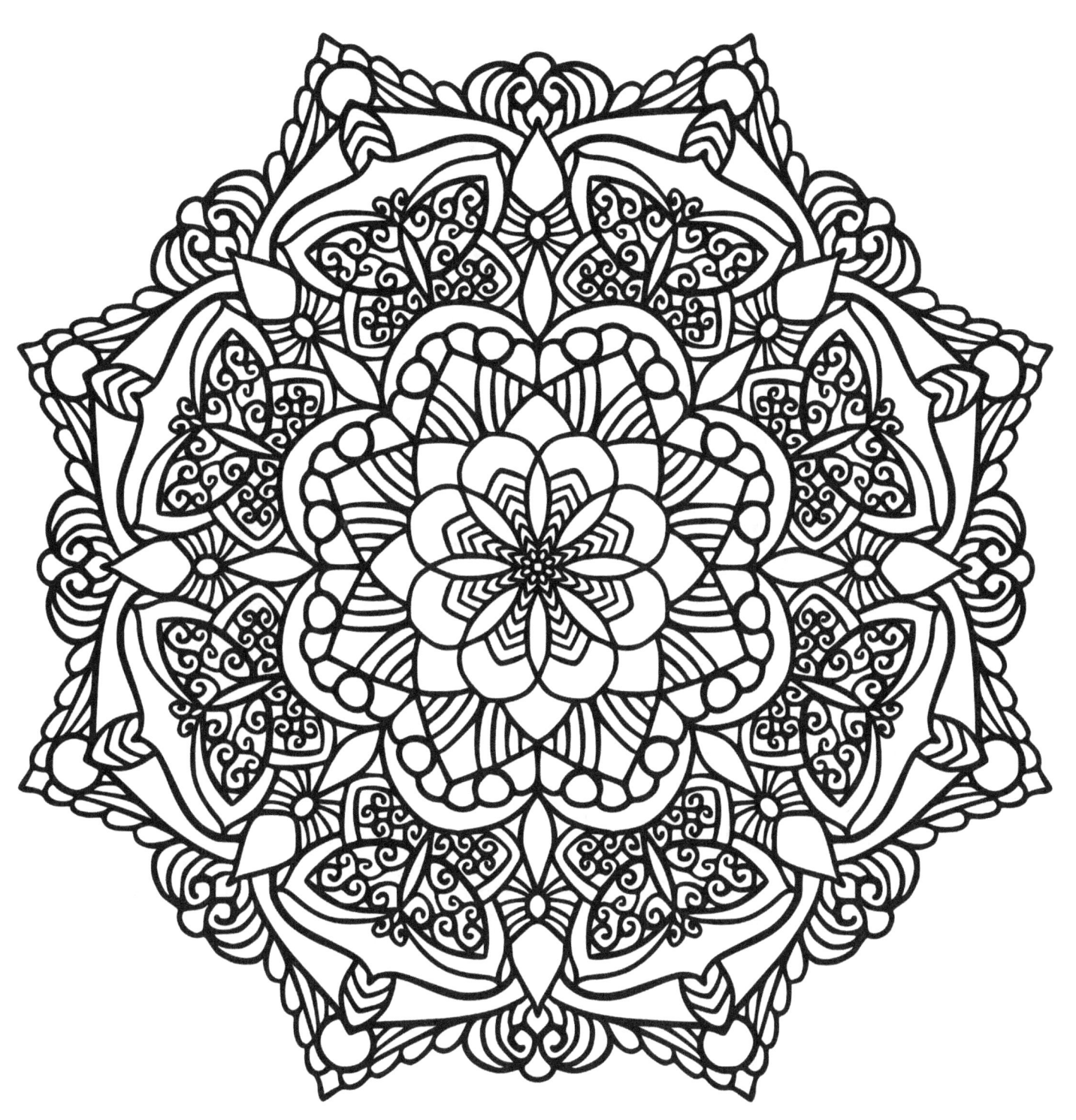

color me loved & supported

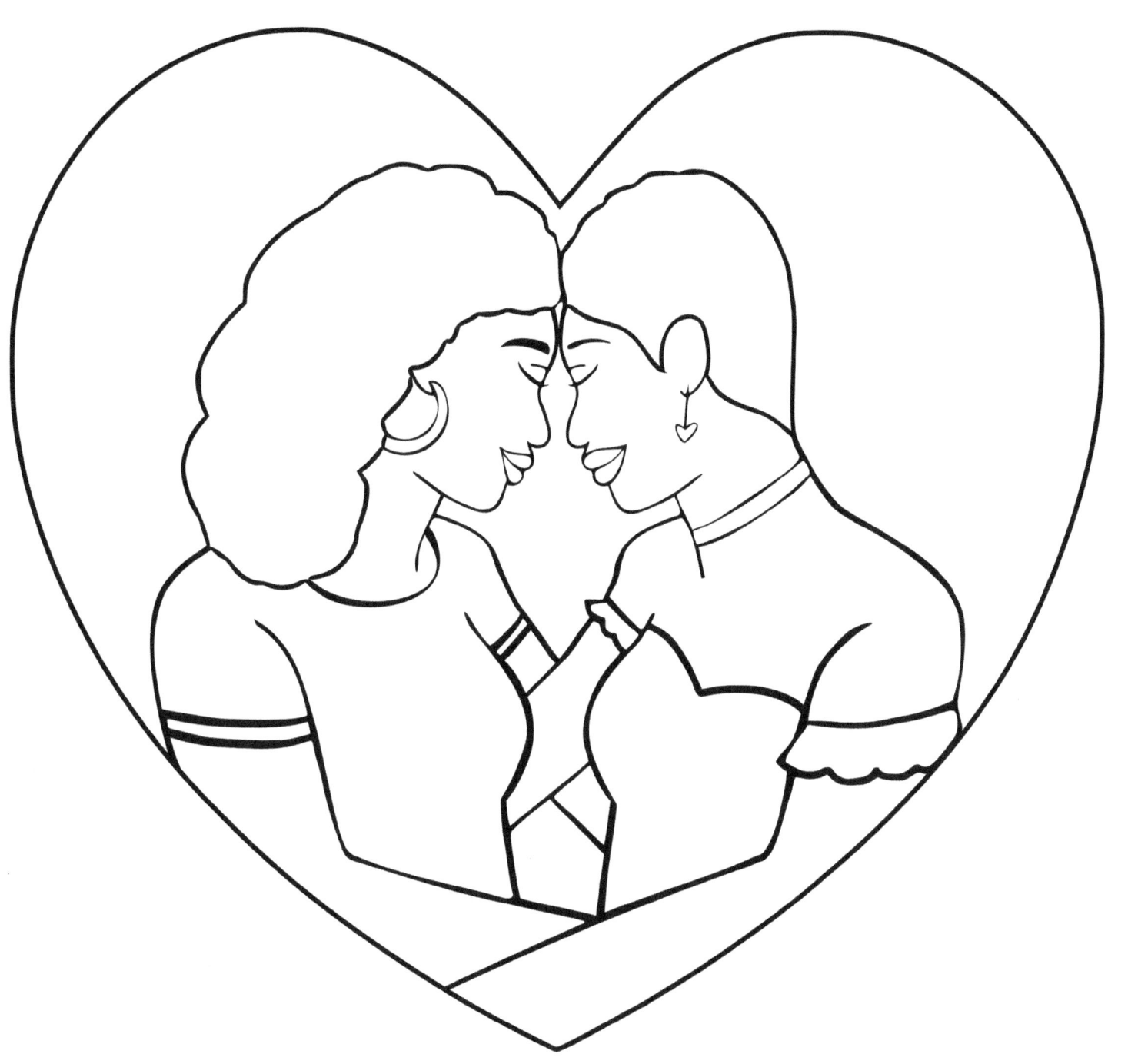

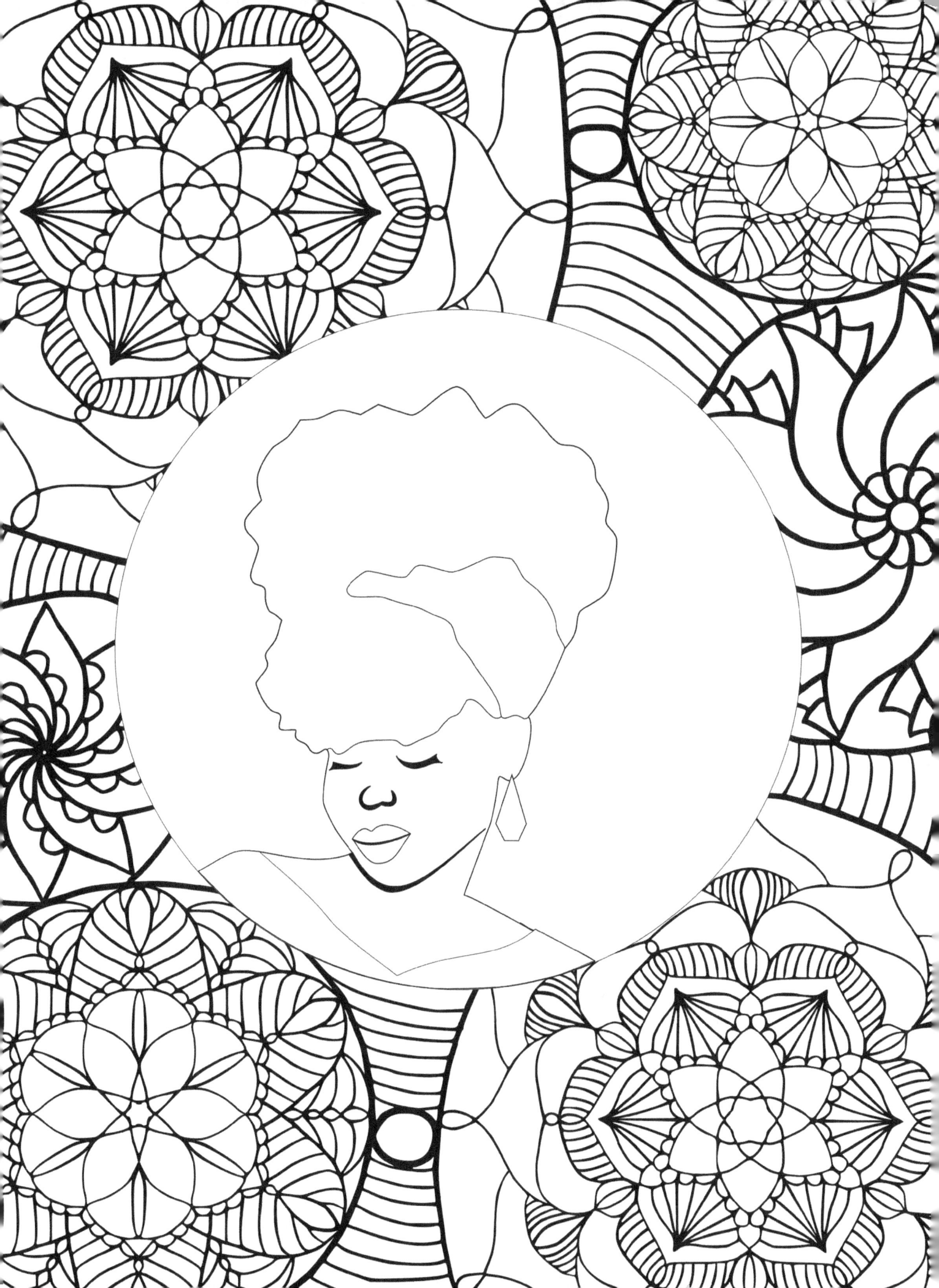

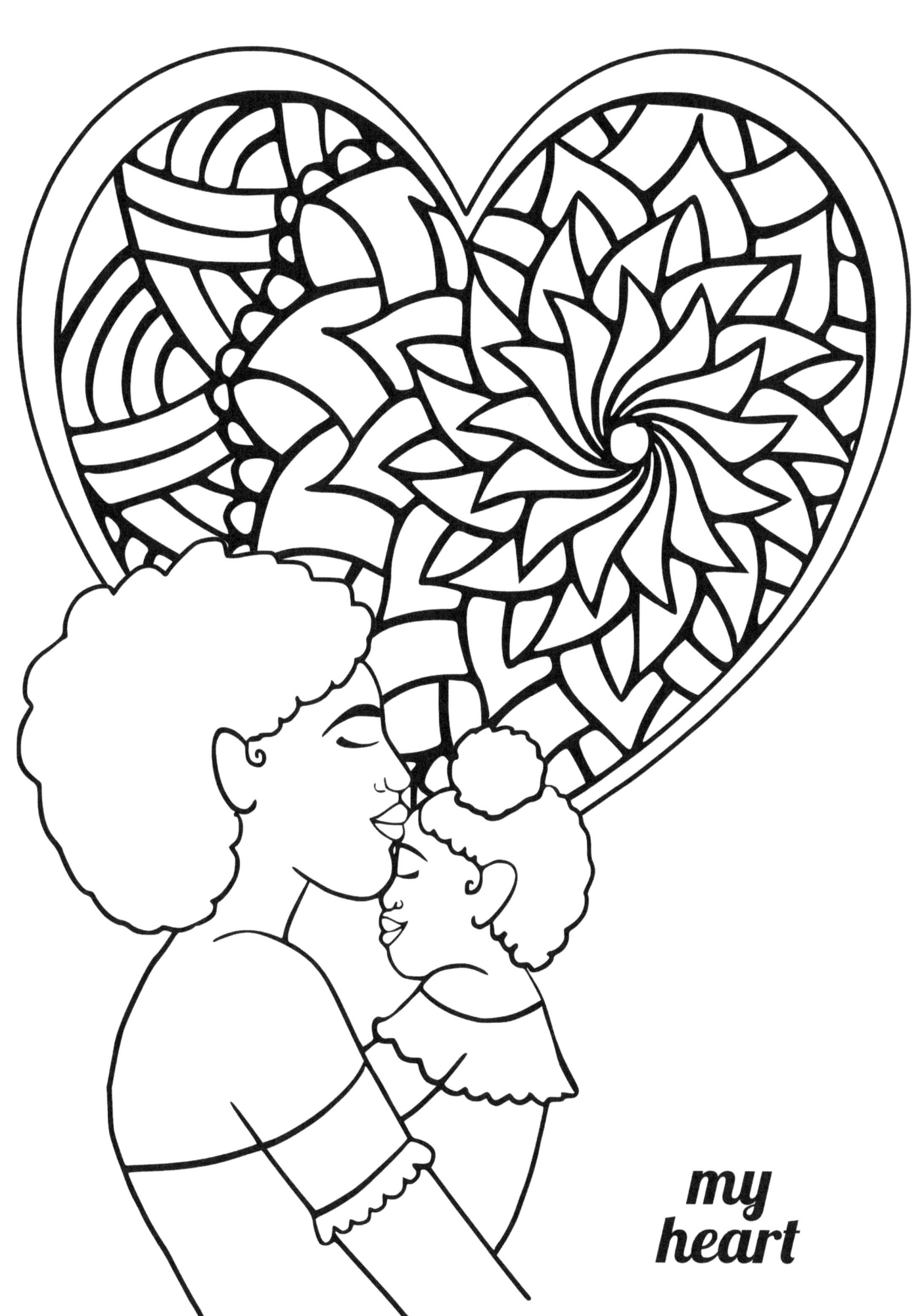

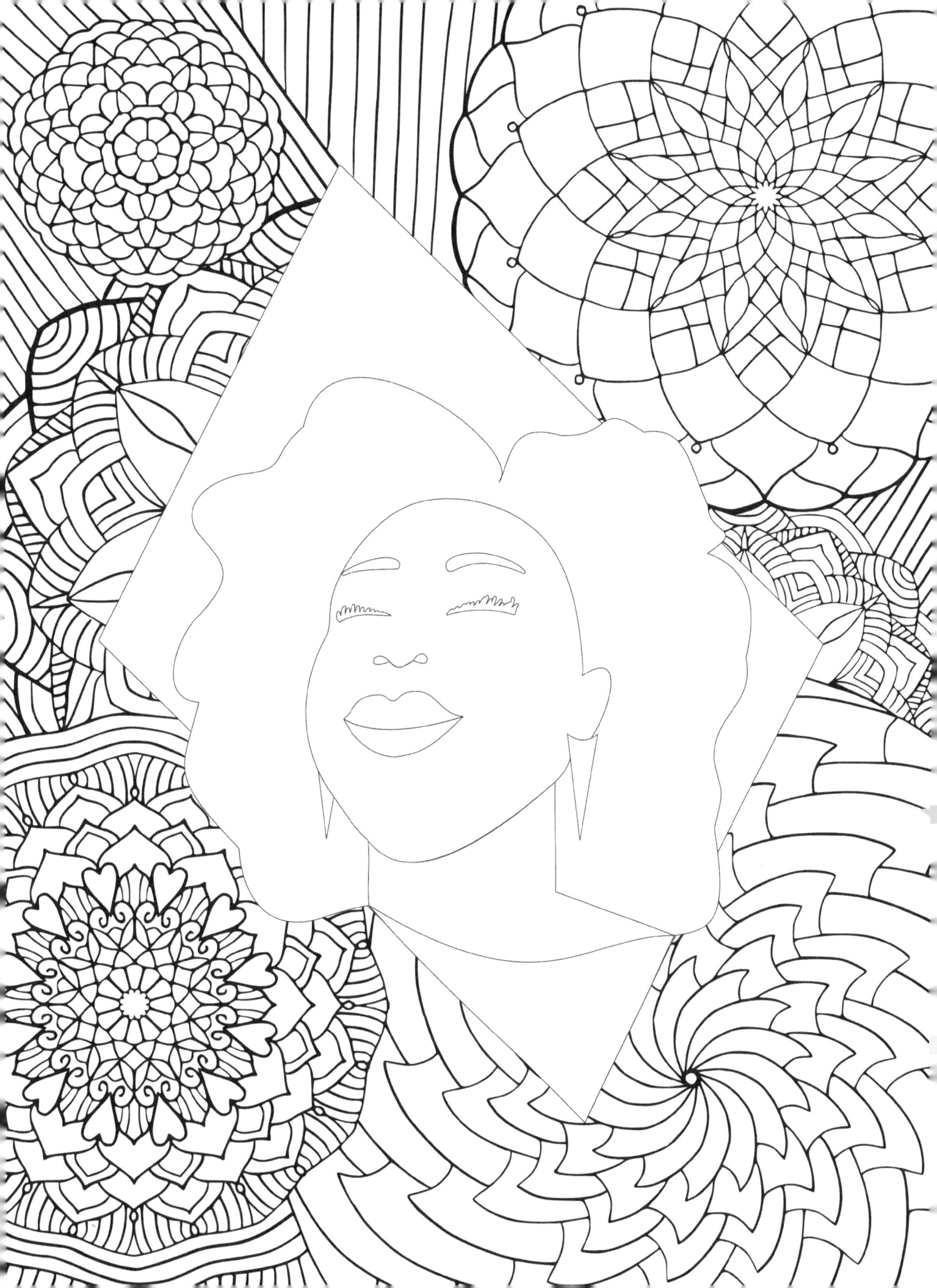

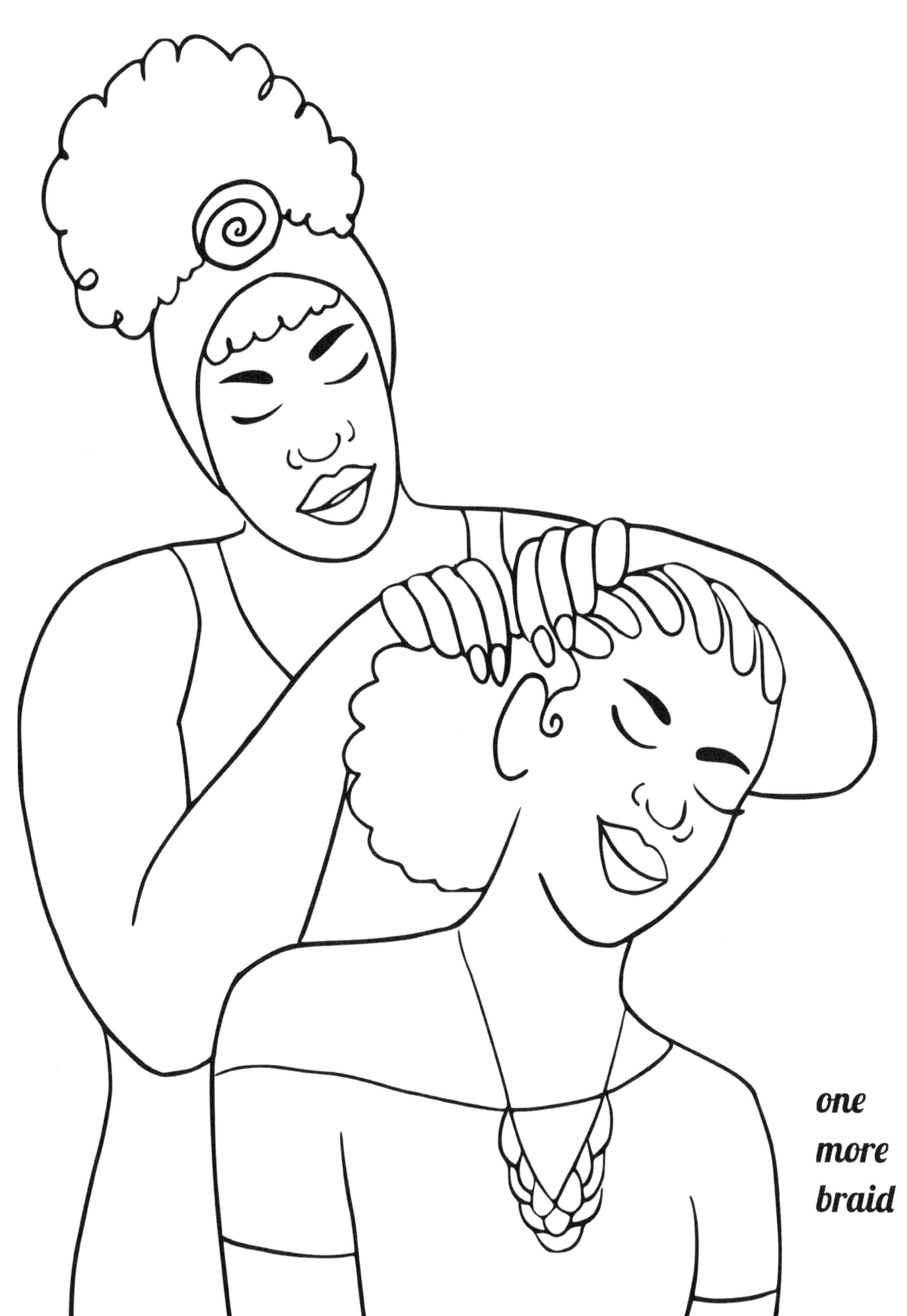

one more braid

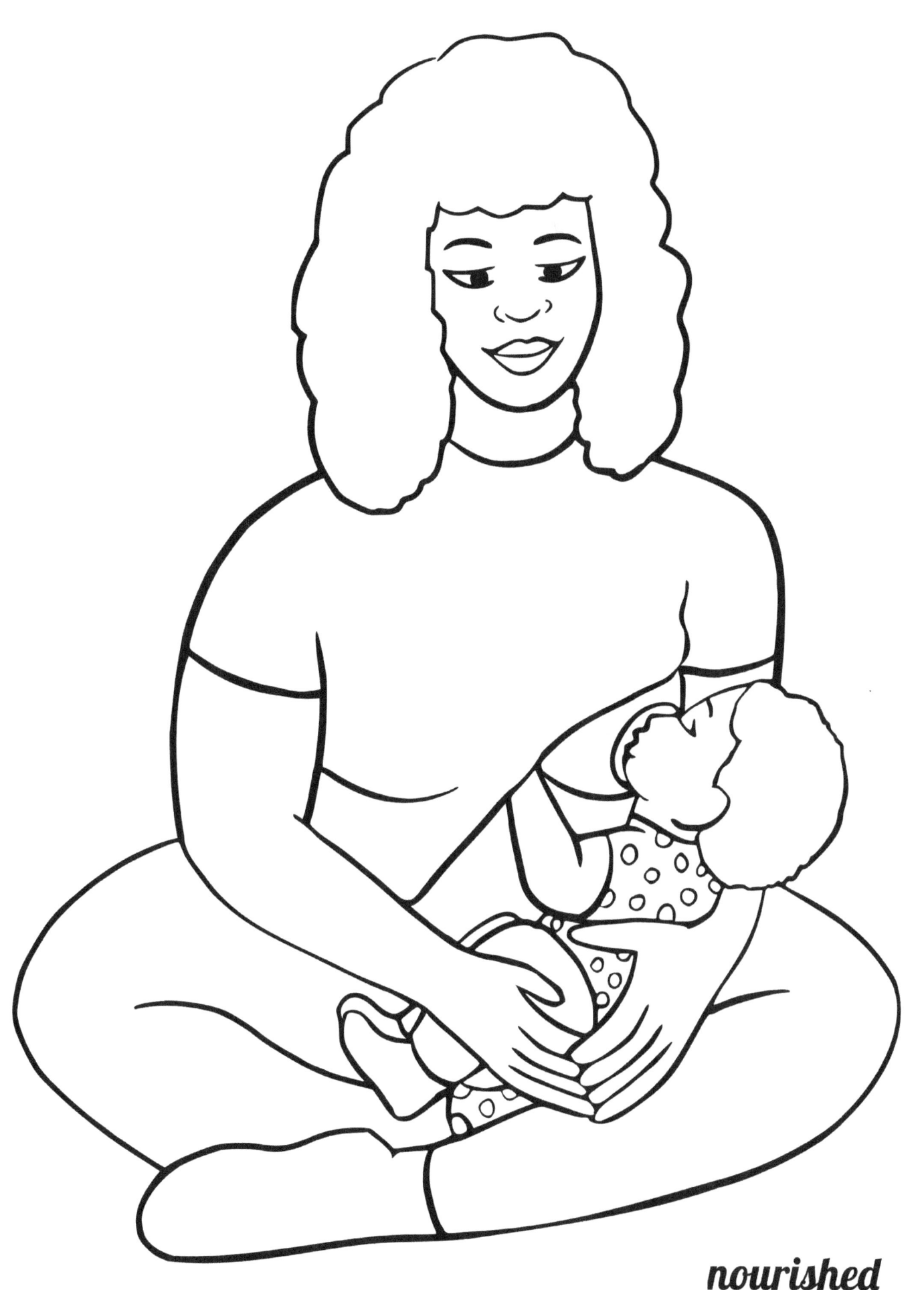

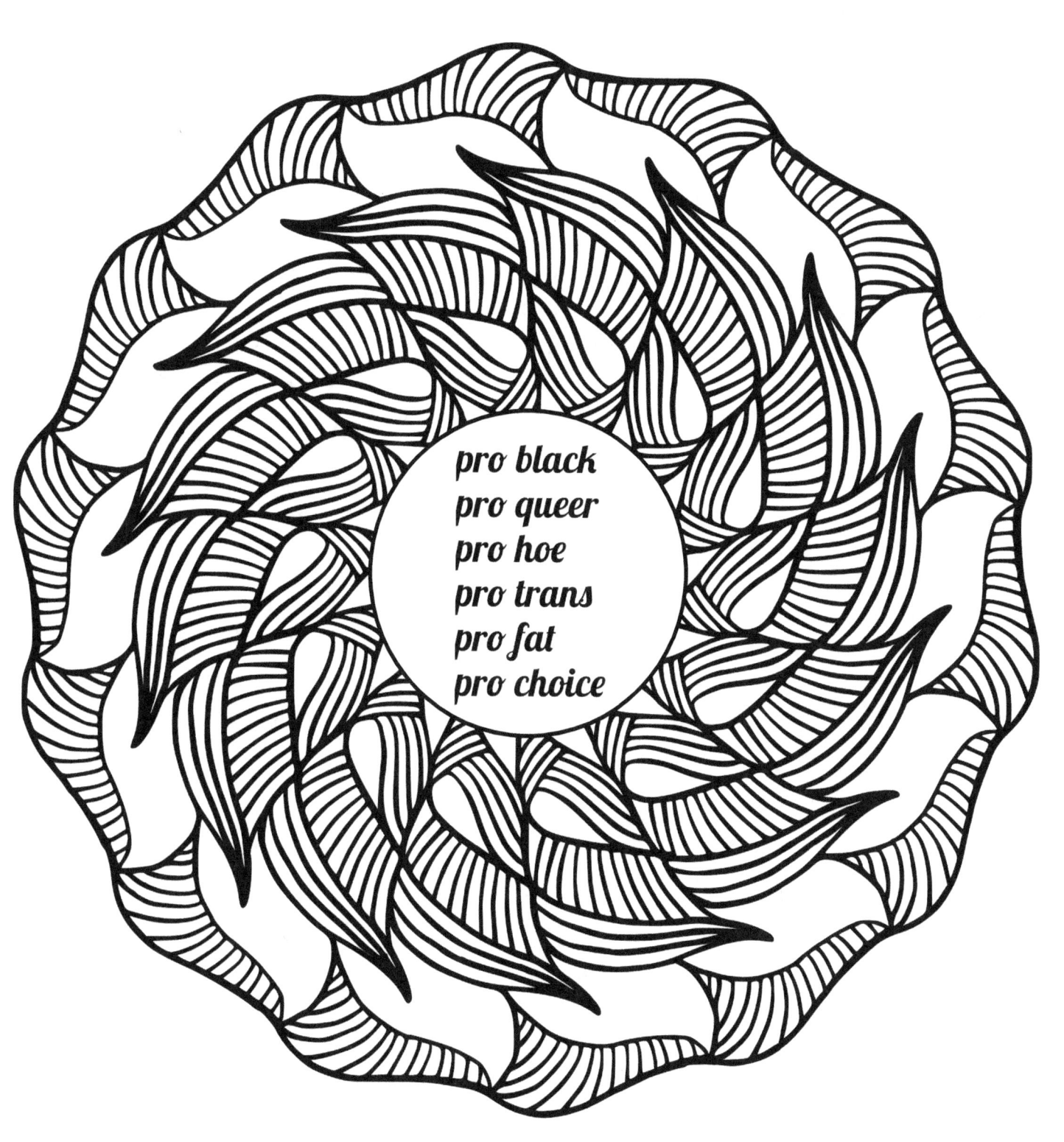

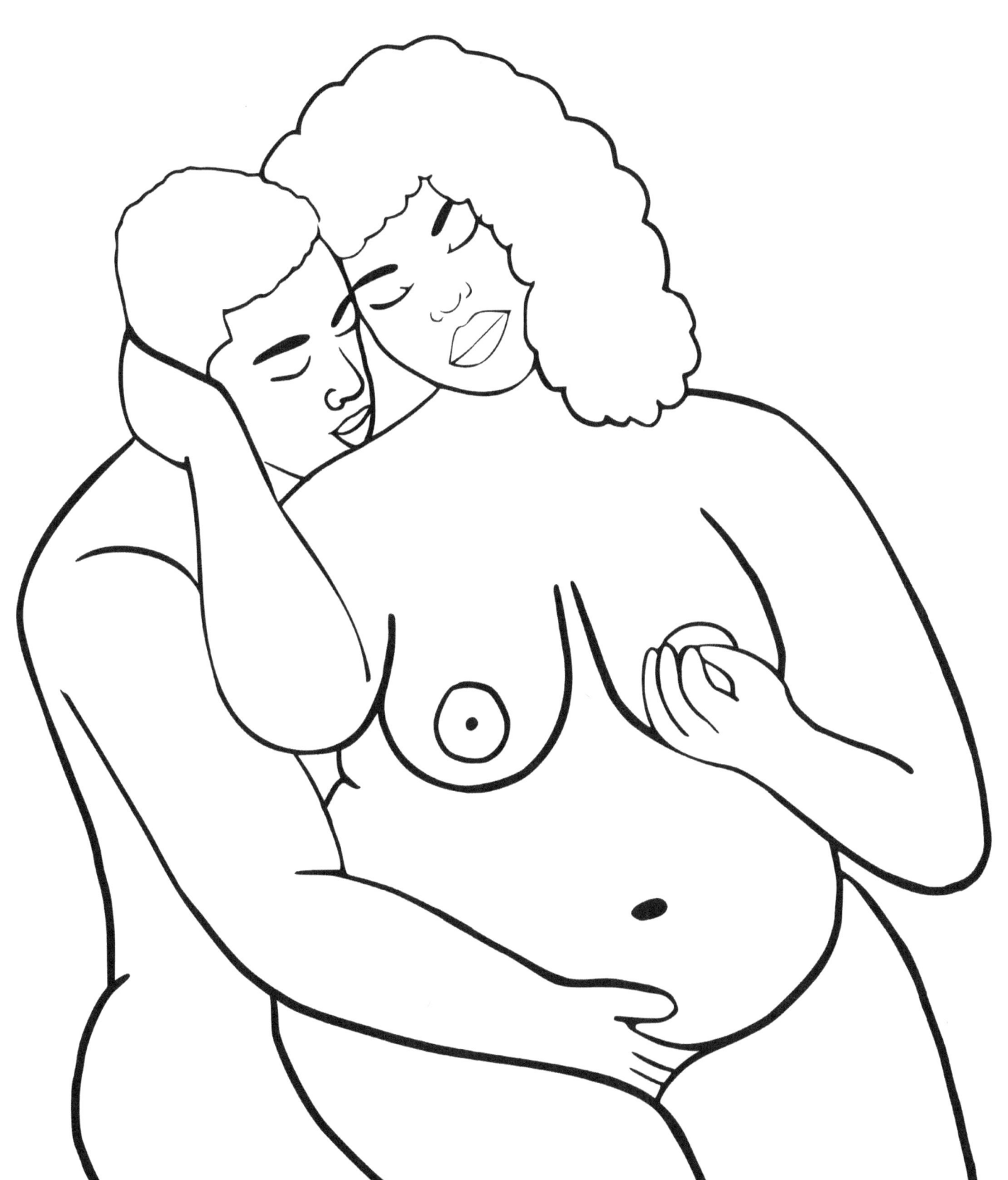

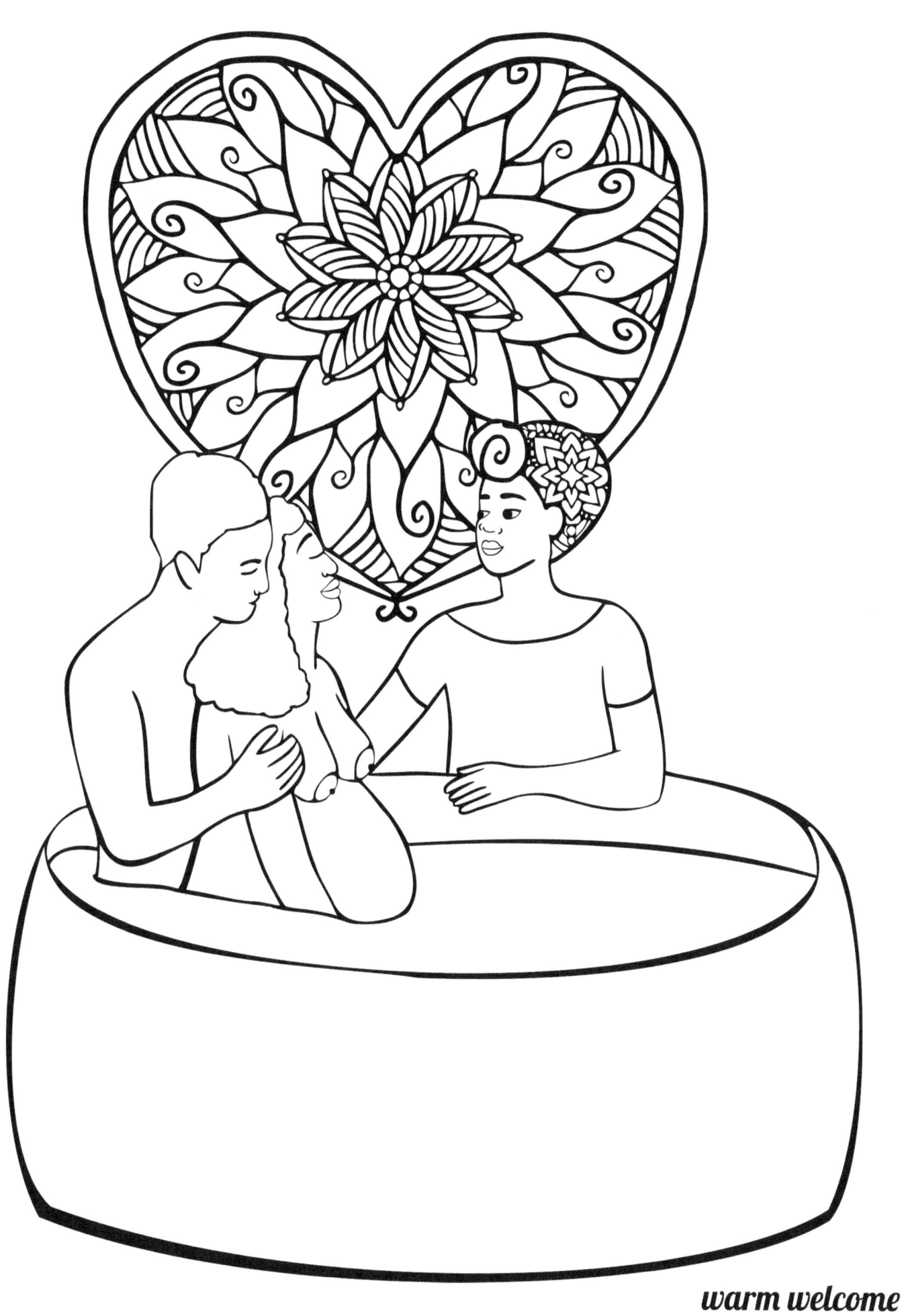

warm welcome

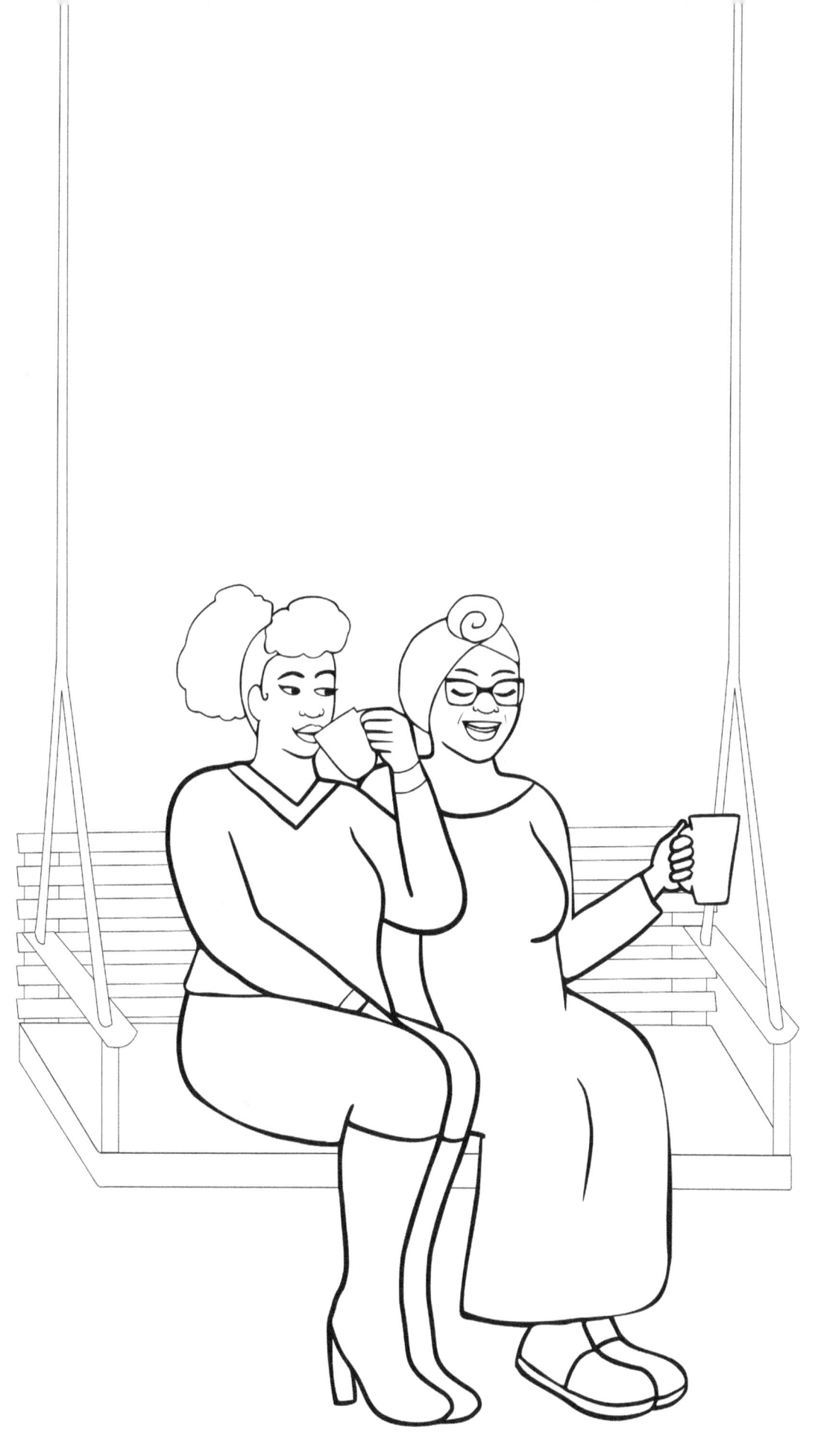

www.ingramcontent.com/pod-product-compliance
Lightning Source LLC
Chambersburg PA
CBHW081429220526
45466CB00008B/2314